Becoming a Playwright

Over thirty years ago David Campton gave up a safe job with the East Midlands Gas Board in order to write for a living. With occasional diversions into acting and directing he has continued to write for a living ever since. He has written over a hundred stage plays, not to mention sketches, radio and TV scripts and short stories. Short pieces appeared in the West End in *One Over the Eight*, *On the Brighter Side*, *Counterpoint* and *Mixed Doubles*. *Jonah* was commissioned for and performed in Chelmsford Cathedral. In 1977 the Japan prize was awarded to his radio script *Look – Sea*. His children's play, *Timesneeze*, was one of three in the repertoire of the Young Vic's first season.

D1392052

Becoming a Playwright

DAVID CAMPTON

ROBERT HALE · LONDON

© David Campton 1992
First published in Great Britain 1992

ISBN 0 7090 4977 3 (cased)
ISBN 0 7090 4990 0 (paperback)

Robert Hale Limited
Clerkenwell House
Clerkenwell Green
London EC1R 0HT

Photoset in Palatino by
Derek Doyle & Associates, Mold, Clwyd.
Printed in Great Britain by
St Edmundsbury Press Ltd, Bury St Edmunds, Suffolk.
Bound by WBC Bookbinders Ltd, Bridgend, Mid-Glamorgan.

Contents

CONTENTS

Introduction

To become a playwright you have to write a play. Obvious? Most elements of playwriting are; but as they seem to be missed by so many aspiring playwrights, perhaps the obvious is the best point at which to start.

A long time ago one of my jobs with a theatre company – along with acting, directing, totting up the takings, preparing press releases, and occasionally sweeping the stage – was the reading of scripts that regularly arrived unannounced. There would be about a hundred a year (after all the company was *very* small). Of these two or three would merit further consideration. Many of the others seemed to have been written by hopefuls who had never been inside a theatre in their lives or, if they had, must have failed to notice what was going on around them. This impression was later strengthened when I found myself asked to judge playwriting competitions and to assess scripts at writing workshops. Which is why in this book I have tried to go back to the very first stages – even as far back as the moment of deciding, 'I want to write a play'.

I know I shall be elaborating on some details that will have experienced writers exclaiming, 'Surely everybody knows that'. Maybe so. But if that is the case why do so many scripts seem to have missed the obvious? (Even occasionally getting produced.) Perhaps we can all benefit from a reminder of basic principles – even echo the successful writer who said, 'I have been doing that all my life, but now I know *why* I'm doing it'.

Becoming a playwright is a continuing process. You learn by doing it. Not only by putting words on to paper (though that is a beginning recommended by Francis

Bacon: 'Writing maketh an exact man'), but by seeing what actors and audiences make of them. The process can be painful, nevertheless it is one that you have to experience for yourself. No one ever became a playwright merely by dreaming of applause.

One of the hazards of enjoying even a slight success is the eruption of an enthusiastic stranger with the idea for a sure-fire success. All you have to do is to write it and then split the resulting fortune fifty-fifty. To such proposals I try to explain, more or less patiently, that the system does not work that way. In any case if the idea is so promising, why doesn't its begetter write the potential block-buster and keep a hundred per cent of the proceeds? More often than not the reply is, 'I don't know the first thing about playwriting'. So I suggest the first step – take a writing implement in your hand and apply it to a sheet of paper.

Of course, even before that, reading this book may not do any harm. It might even help.

I would like to thank Christopher Fry for the use of lines from *The Lady's Not For Burning*.

1 In the Beginning

Good news! Anyone can write a play. Not necessarily a masterpiece: to write a masterpiece needs application and/or special aptitude. Some writers seem to have been born with an instinctive feel for the medium, apparent even in apprentice efforts. In their hands the process seems to be not so much the manipulation of rules as a method of expression as natural as breathing. Even the best playwrights, though, need to develop their powers: *Widowers' Houses* is a long way from *Arms and the Man*, and Ayckbourn's *Relatively Speaking* was not his first play but his sixth – which may lend hope to all those who feel the need for directions in play construction. However, to repeat: anyone can write a play. It is not even necessary to make marks on paper. Children are making up plays all the time. So do not feel there is anything mysterious or esoteric about technique. Just as correct exercises can work wonders for seven-stone weaklings, so an understanding and practice of basic principles can eventually help to bring forth a workable script.

These principles are quite simple. When Stephen Joseph came to the chapter on lighting in the book he was writing on theatre-in-the-round he wrote, 'The beam of light should strike the object it is illuminating at an angle of forty-five degrees'. Then he stopped. 'What more is there to say?' he asked me. 'Once you've grasped that, the rest follows.'

I now face a similar difficulty. The basic principles of dramatic writing can be written on a thumb nail; and once they have been grasped, the rest follows. All else is a matter of dotting an 'i' here or crossing a 't' there. Styles and superficialities may change, but the qualities that make for a good play remain constant.

A good play is not necessarily the same as a successful play. Nothing here or hereafter will tell anyone how to achieve even a three-night run with their local drama society, let alone a fortune in the West End or on Broadway. That is part of *selling* a play which needs luck and a knowledge of local conditions, and more luck with all the right factors coming together at the same time; but luck most of all.

Without luck a very good play can die in a bottom drawer (a play, being a perishable commodity, can date very quickly); while with luck even a very bad play can run for years. It is not for mortals to command success, but by writing as well as we are able, we may at least feel virtuously that we deserve it.

Playwriting *can* be learned. (Some will learn quicker than others, of course, and in some cases the learning process may be found to be so slow and painful, the desired results so long delayed, that they will give up before achieving any breakthrough.) I have in my time been involved with classes, workshops and courses and have welcomed achievement in what at first seemed to be hopeless cases, the rawest beginners with nothing on their side but eagerness. Occasionally re-reading my own earliest efforts, I have been appalled. If today I were offered those fumbling attempts by a student, I should be tempted to advise taking up something more suited to those talents – such as digging holes. It took over ten years, writing as well as I knew how, before anything of mine reached the stage – and that was a tiny sketch, directed and acted by myself for an end-of-term party. Which is why I feel that no one should be discouraged, belittled or turned away. If I had despaired after only nine years, I should not be earning my living from writing today.

I can remember in those days searching for a magic formula, like an alchemist's philosopher's stone. I believed there must be some trick that would turn an unbroken line of rejections into instant acceptances. There is, of course, neither trick nor magic – in fact I still have rejections (one not so long ago began, 'Mr Campton must be mad'). Instead there is more likely to be a slowly dawning awareness of what everyone has been saying for a very long time. In those days I read every book on writing that I could lay my hands on. Some of these were good, and even today (when fashions in the theatre have changed) contain much that is relevant. Towards the most sound advice in them I found myself saying, 'But that is obvious. I know that already'. How odd that, knowing so much, I was achieving so little! Hardly surprising that I continued to search for a touchstone as out of reach as any alchemist's. Fortunately my experiments for turning lead into gold involved nothing more drastic than boring friends in my drama group with inadequate inventions. Over the years these must have shown some improvement, because at last there came a suggestion that at the Christmas get-together I might like to 'put on something to fill in the time while the cups and saucers were being washed'.

That first commission started a trend. Almost everything I have written since then has been to order – or at least for a particular organization with a production in mind, from the local Women's Institute to the BBC. Perhaps my first important discovery, so obvious as to go for a long time unrecognized, was that playwriting is a practical subject and that the best way to find out how is to do it. As with sex there are any number of manuals giving instructions on how to set about the job, but in the end there is no alternative to becoming personally involved.

My advice to any aspiring playwright is to join a dramatic society. I started by joining two. One concentrated on reproducing West End successes, while the other's choice of play tended towards the bizarre. For several years I bounced between *George and Margaret* or *Ladies in Retirement* and *Agamemnon* or *The Ascent of F6*, with fewer breaks between shows than if I had been working in a regular repertory company. My parts varied from such leads as Figaro and Harpagon to two lines of the 'carriage awaits' variety. It was all valuable experience. In spite of TV there are still enough amateur companies flourishing to give anybody the chance to join at least one of them. As a last resort form your own group. A play on the stage is worth ten in the book for anyone studying any aspect of the theatre, if only because the printed page misses the other elements vital to the dramatic experience – actors and audience.

If you cannot act, or hammer nails, or paint, or prompt (and you never know what you can do until you try) at least you can join the audience. See plays in performance: in the village or school hall as well as in the professional theatre. And remember that as much can be gleaned from a disaster as from a smash hit – if only by learning what *not* to do.

Read plays too. Not merely the latest from London or New York: take in as many periods and countries as you can. A play takes about the same length of time to read as an average short story, so there is no reason why you should not manage one a day; particularly if you have much travelling to do. With some experience of theatre-going it is possible to develop what Lawrence Langer called 'a theatre in your head', mentally going some way towards making up for the lack of those living collaborators. There is much to be gained from noting how the greats, from Aeschylus to Brecht, went about their work. In particular consider what it is that raised them to eminence in their own time and gives them life even today.

On a rather lower plane however, let us ask what it is that we, ordinary, run-of-the-mill, working playwrights make. What is this thing called a play? In order to build a better mousetrap a desirable first step must surely be to decide what mousetraps are for and how they function. What is it that an audience pays for and cannot buy anywhere else?

A story? Most plays tell a story. On the most elementary level an audience likes to ask 'what happens next?'. It is no accident that the most memorable plays have a strong story-line. Yet, if it is *only* a story we hanker for, there is nothing to keep us from curling up with a good book. Literature – to say nothing of the current best-seller list – offers a host of good stories. Why make the effort (sometimes considerable in terms of cash and transport) to visit a playhouse? Because there we get something more than a story. The fiction comes to life, happening before our eyes. Even on the crudest stage with cobbled-up scenery there is an element of spectacle.

Spectacle has considerable drawing power. From time to time the visual element has actually dominated the stage. (Ben Jonson fell out with Inigo Jones when he felt that the set designer was taking the attention of the audience from his words.) In the nineteenth century the scene painter was prominently credited on the playbill, often given more prominence than the author. In the heyday of Drury Lane melodrama, races were staged, ships blew up, volcanos erupted. A spectacular production can still attract queues to the box office. It may be worth noting, though, that one of the most expensive spectacles to reach Broadway (an adaptation of *Frankenstein* – not mine!) cost over £1,000,000 for the special effects, and closed after one performance. The producers had neglected to ensure that the play matched the picture.

The colour and movement of Trooping the Colour, the Edinburgh Tattoo or even a local rag day procession draws enthusiastic crowds; but the pleasure derived from pageantry is of a different order from involvement in a play. Could it be that the missing element is doubt? Every movement in a big parade is carefully planned. Nothing (we trust) can go wrong. Order is of the essence. We must look elsewhere for conflict.

The sports field for instance. Here is conflict enough. With luck, and sides evenly matched, the issue will be in doubt until the last second. (Louis MacNeice once said that he would rather see a good rugger match than *Oedipus Rex* because he knew already how *Oedipus* was going to end.) Yet even in this sports-conscious country more people go to the theatre than to football matches. One can go to both of course – enjoyment is not exclusive. But what does the theatre have that Wimbledon, Lords and Wembley do not? Language perhaps? The spoken word?

Shaw in his day as a dramatic critic wondered why people did not go to church rather than the theatre. The surroundings were more comfortable and the entertainment superior. (Always remembering that the 1890s were the heyday of the popular preacher and that Shaw himself derived more pleasure from a well-delivered sermon than from a flimsy comedy or mindless melodrama.) The preacher, the political orator, the poetry reciter and the lecturer (with or without visual aids) use a combination of the resources of actor and playwright, such as tone of voice, gesture and choice of words to influence their audiences, convey information or, more importantly, produce a mass reaction. As Shaw noted, this reaction can be very like that experienced in a theatre. In fact at times there is a close resemblance to a one-man show. Playwrights have written speeches, verse and probably sermons: clergymen, MPs and poets have certainly written plays.

A play combines all those elements of story-line, suspense, spectacle and language to arouse an emotional response in the audience – laughter, tears, pity, indignation etc. – but finally, and most importantly a release of those emotions. (Could this final relief be the reason why, after the final fall of the curtain, theatre-goers seldom go on the rampage, committing acts of vandalism?) A commonplace analogy is the stretching and releasing of a rubber band. Tension is created by involving us *en masse* in the problems of characters on stage, and by manipulating the events that lead to a major climax. As the issues are resolved (for better or worse, happily or unhappily, but resolved) then the tension is released.

In that manipulation of events and characters to produce an effect on the audience lies the art of playwriting. Never underrate your audience. The audience is the playwright's ultimate reason for existing. Writing a play without considering the audience is like shooting arrows without a target – useful as exercise maybe, but in the last analysis pointless.

What follows will be mainly given to considering that manipulation. Ways and means will be reviewed under various headings – outlines, scenarios, characters, dialogue and so on. This is for convenience, because an attempt to swallow too much too quickly results in dyspepsia.

At the same time it should never be forgotten that all aspects of writing are related, and the creative impulse does not necessarily take any notice of a table of contents.

An original idea may come in the form of a situation, which involves, perhaps, speaking dialogue – such as 'Do not strike that man: he is your father!' (around which Wilde may have constructed *A Woman of No Importance*). The idea may come in the form of a character, and characters are certainly part of the internal structure of a play; but a character, even as introspective as Hamlet, has to be presented in terms of action. The whole play may even flash into your mind (as Mozart is reputed to have conceived symphonies) complete with costumes, settings, moves and sound effects.

However a check-list of points to consider can do no harm. It may even prove useful in later stages when revision is called for, or when you get that feeling of something being wrong but you cannot put your finger on it. I have in my time suffered from writers' block, when I become incapable of putting one word next to another – and attempts to force the pace merely produced a mess that flew straight into the waste-paper basket. Nearly always I have traced this block to a technical problem with which my subconscious was wrestling, preventing my pressing forward until it had been solved. One notable example was in the one-act *But Not Here*. I had reached page 15 when the characters went on strike and would neither move nor speak. I put the play aside and went back to it several months later. On re-reading it I realized that the play actually *began* on page 15. Once those first pages had been put aside (much of the material was incorporated later) the play rattled on merrily to its end.

Sooner or later we must all become involved in the process of actually getting words on to paper – even those who command dictating machines and secretaries. So before going any further some consideration of working methods may not come amiss. It has truly been said that one writer's routine is another's nervous breakdown. Some write little and often; some make a frantic dash when deadlines are looming. Personally I should advise a beginner to opt for the little and often approach. Daydreaming is so easy, and the act of forcing a reluctant pen to move can be such drudgery that it is always as well to establish good habits in one's early days. Having fallen into some bad habits myself, I now frequently find that I have to deceive my conscious mind into believing that I am not really working at all. Consequently, what amounts in the end to a first draft, is often jotted down in snatches on odd scraps of paper, which are eventually swept together for revision. These days, when I am a so-called full-time writer, I find that I am achieving (in quantity at least) far less than when I worked in an office. In those days this was fortunately within walking distance of home – twenty minutes there and twenty minutes back twice a day. That eighty minutes of pedestrian cogitation gave me the chance to work out what I should be doing when I next sat down with an exercise book. Consequently when I did sit down I was seldom at a loss for words, and writing time was used exclusively for that purpose. No doodling or pencil chewing. I set aside half an hour before setting out in the morning, half an hour at midday (out of the ninety minutes allowed for lunch) and half an hour after tea, before dashing off to rehearsal. There were occasional complaints from my family who, seeing me so seldom, would occasionally ask if I still lived in the district; but under that regime of an hour and a half per day, the pages mounted up. The quality may not have been outstanding but that way I wrote my first five one-act plays to be published and my first two full-length plays to be professionally produced. After which I gave up my job. (Sometimes wondering since whether I made the right decision.)

Time is needed for writing. Some professional writers talk of 'buying time', that is writing to make the money on which to live while they get down to the risky project they have set their heart on. Time can be made and the simplest way, if your living has to be earned elsewhere, is to devote a short but regular period to writing each day. (Without cheating, because in this business you can only be cheating yourself.) One page of 250 words each day becomes a novel-length manuscript by the end of a year. That is the equivalent in words of at least two full-length plays or six one-acts. Don't forget those long walks, though, in which much of my thinking was done and my material organized.

Different writers have different ways of organizing their material. Taking those encouraging words 'Act One – Scene One' as the starting point, there are almost as many ways of arriving at it as there are writers.

Some keep voluminous notebooks. Those of Somerset Maugham and Henry James are certainly worth reading if only for spotting the entries in which lurk the ideas that later became well-known stories and plays; the few words that grew into full-scale works. Henry James was fond of making lists of characters and places (some of them were eventually used). J.M. Barrie noted the idea of a young mother's ghost unable to recognize her child because he had grown up, twenty years before writing *Mary Rose*. (The seed of a play can take a long time to germinate.)

Personally I am always jotting down titles and single sentence notions on scraps of paper which, when my desk top becomes too cluttered, I pack into boxes. From time to time I sort through these collections, wondering why I ever considered such fragments as 'It crawls out of the river' or 'The Down Line' worth recording. Obviously they meant more to me at the time. Other suggestions are more detailed, even running to several pages. Why didn't I set to work on them there and then? Well, sometimes I was in the middle of another project. (Sometimes they grew out of that other project.) Some were just not ready to be written. More than once I have been forced to abandon work in progress (temporarily, if not permanently) because the idea itself was just not ready to be born. The notion that the stuff of creative writing may have a life of its own sounds fanciful (reminding one of the characters in a story who take over their author – and please do not write that old chestnut again!) but I have come to respect it. So into the file they went until they clamoured to be let out, or were pressed into service. From time to time urgent requests have come winging out of the blue. 'Can you let me have a script by yesterday?' At which my mind has a tendency to become blank. On such occasions my idea boxes have proved invaluable.

When I actually come to write a play, I tend to fill pages with notes – often disjointed and even irrelevant, on the background to and the relationships between characters.

These notes may be used or scrapped as necessary. (A warning here, which may be repeated later: do not presume that everything turned up during preliminary excavations must necessarily be incorporated into the work in hand. Selection and rejection are part of the process.) From these notes, though, the play takes shape.

Although some writers manage without a detailed blueprint, most know where they are going before they start out. Somerset Maugham for instance would be sure of the curtain line of each act and work towards that, even though the rest of the action existed only at the back of his mind. From their own remarks Tennessee Williams and Peter Terson would seem to sit down at their typewriters in order to find out what they are going to write. (Follow their example if you have a large enough waste-paper basket for all the false starts.) G.B.S. insisted that he would start at the top of a page without the slightest inkling of what was going to happen by the bottom of it. Bear in mind, though, that he did not include phonetics in his attack on medical practice, nor bring his ideas on longevity into the Salvation Army. He was always aware of his objective, even though he relied upon a homing instinct to get him there. (Sometimes that failed him: read in his letters of the trouble he had with the ending of *Major Barbara*.)

Some writers prepare a very detailed scenario. (The scenario of Edward Knobloch's *Kismet* is almost as long as the finished play.) I certainly did this in my very young days, partly because a scenario showed up basic faults in construction before too much work had been done, possibly reducing the amount of rewriting; and partly because, with basic construction settled, I could concentrate more on details of dialogue and characterization.

A scenario, though, should never be allowed to put characters into strait-jackets. They must develop minds and lives of their own; as and when they do so, be prepared to change course.

Whatever approach to work a writer feels most comfortable with, it is most unusual to start with no notion at all of what is to follow. This can be a great temptation from time to time, especially when the necessary spark has been absent for some time and shows no sign of ever being struck again. If you have never spent frustrating hours staring as it were into an awful void, and recalling tales of writers being written out, you can count yourself lucky. Nevertheless the vague feeling of wanting to write a play with no more inspiration than that to back it up, is the most dangerous of starting points: if only because it leaves you wide open to plagiarism – remembering rather than creating. (Read in William Archer's *Playmaking* how in an idle afternoon he devised the outline of an entirely new play – only to realize after sober reflection that he had just reconstructed *Hedda Gabler*.) Wanting to write a play is not quite enough. You must have a play to write.

When you know where you are going, you can take the next step. But however it may come, and whatever it may look like, you cannot start without an idea. So where is it to come from?

2   The Very Idea

Many years ago, while at school studying organic chemistry, I was taught that crystals will not form without something to start them. That something may be as apparently insignificant as a speck of dust, or even a scratch on the side of a glass flask, but without it there will be no crystal. That is almost all I do remember of organic chemistry and it might have stuck in my mind because of its relevance to playwriting (in which I was also taking my first tentative steps). Every play needs a speck or a scratch around which it can form.

John Van Druten in *Playwright at Work*, the autobiographical account of his working methods, is more biological. He writes, 'All the ideas started tiny, as one cell only, and the cell grew until it became a play.'

Harold Pinter is on record as having written the line, 'What have you done with the scissors?' and then carried on with *The Homecoming* from there.

O'Neill started *The Emperor Jones* with the sound of a tom-tom; the insistent beat of an African drum was the seed from which that play grew.

Speaking for myself, I saw an old lady muffled to her eyebrows in a November gale, almost leaning against the wind, who developed into the vengeful ghost of *I'm Sorry, Mrs Baxter*. I do not know where the visual image came from of a soldier, bearing on his own body all the wounds he had ever inflicted on anyone else; but I saw that stage picture in my mind's eye and devised *Soldier from the Wars Returning* (which later went on to the West End) in which to set it. Of his play *After All*, Van Druten writes: 'I was driving in a taxi past the college where my mother used to go. I saw the girls arriving there, and I can remember thinking: "Mother as a girl. I wonder if she ever thought of me then". That may not sound like a very good beginning for a play, but it was how that one started, and the remark stayed in the script.' One cell. One spark. The nucleus.

But where to find that cell, spark or nucleus – that essential idea?

There is in fact only one place from which an idea can come: from inside yourself. Obvious, considering how all perceptions and feelings about this world (or even the next) are filtered through one's own senses – perhaps with the acknowledgement that there may be another in addition to the accepted five. Your own self and nobody else's.

Another person's experiences can only be used creatively by relating them to one's own. Your bright-eyed heroine may proclaim ecstatically that she is in love, but you can only have an inkling of what she feels by recollecting your own state of mind when similarly affected. This does not mean that, in order to write about a painful accident or the loss of a love, one should deliberately break a leg or an engagement: we are capable of comparing one experience with another, of reconstructing sensations or linking emotions. Indeed it is only by this process that rapport can in the end be established with an audience. Which may be one reason why some plays are untranslatable.

There may well be some emotions difficult to identify with. Once commissioned to write a play about teenage vandals, I could not myself feel any sense of fun in wanton destruction and so took a long time to get under the skin of the characters. I managed in the end by going back to the enjoyment I felt (when very young) of whacking off the heads of thistles with a walking-stick.

We are assisted in our attempts to communicate by the fact that most of us living today share a great deal of common experience. We read from the same limited selection of newspapers, watch the same television programmes, eat the same foods, are affected by the same government policies (either approvingly or disapprovingly), even – allowing for the vagaries of fashion – wear roughly similar clothes. All of which helps towards communication – especially useful if one happens to be in the communication business, as writers are. So when we 'talk of horses' (or of crunching breakfast cereal or swearing at a jammed zip) most audiences will know what we have in mind.

Apart from providing inexhaustible material for soap opera, this shared experience of day-to-day pleasures and frustrations is one of the reasons why playwriting styles tend to come in waves. The minds of those living at the same time and in the same place tend to be occupied by the same topics. Current preoccupations seem to be sex (straight and reversible), human rights (establishing that women and other races are also human) and politics (particularly of protest). Unfortunately this has also led to a plethora of plays in which rather mushy propaganda has taken precedence over more important requirements of playwriting, such as characterization and construction.

In the late fifties a group of up-and-coming playwrights appeared on the cover of the magazine *Encore*. The group included John Mortimer, Harold Pinter, N.F. Simpson, Ann Jellicoe, Bernard Kops and others including myself. Our voices were individual – not even the laziest critic could confuse John Mortimer with N.F. Simpson or Harold Pinter with Ann Jellicoe – yet there was a link between us. Lazy critics did suggest that we had all been influenced by Beckett and Ionesco. Even lazier critics suggested that we had all been influenced by each other: which considering most of us came together for the first time when the photograph was taken, was more absurd than most of our plays. What we *did* have in common was the period in which we were all living. After growing up through the war and immediate post-war years, what young writer could still turn out plays like Dodie Smith?

Just as no two people have identical fingerprints, so not even twins can have exactly the same memories. And memories, which are the stuff of dreams, are also the stuff of fiction. Even when they are memories of other stories heard long before. *Dick Whittington* and *Three Little Pigs* are as much a part of our lives as our Auntie Maud, who liked her little tipple and smelled of peppermint. In spite of that large area of shared experience, each of us is unique; each person's attitude to the world in which they live has to be theirs alone.

Which is why similar starting points should produce totally contrasting plays. Imagine the difference in results if Tennessee Williams, Pinter, Willy Russell or Ayckbourn all decided to adapt *Cinderella*. When you come to put words on paper, you are on your own.

So, because in all creative writing autobiography is of the essence, why not start by searching your own past for inspiration? There is material even in the most retired existence passed in the quietest backwater.

I once suggested to a director that I may have had too little experience of Life (with that capital L) and perhaps I should take up more unusual jobs in other parts of the world. His reply was a firm, 'Nonsense'. He pointed out that in the thirty years I had already lived, I had already experienced enough to keep me writing for the next thirty. Much later I was called abroad on business, an experience confirming that the Campton who watched the sun go down over Kuala Lumpur was exactly the same Campton who had watched it come up over Leicester. It was the same sun, too.

Make the most of yourself. There must have been something in your life that left a marked impression. What was it? It may have been a major turning point – a birth, death or marriage. On the other hand, and more likely, it may have been something as apparently trivial as the beastly boy next door potting sparrows with his airgun, or the not-so-sober stranger who insisted on sharing a train compartment and his troubles, or merely the sight of a cake ablaze with candles. If such as these can be called to mind years later, then they must have significance for you. They are there waiting to be used.

For instance backgrounds.... Over my father's shop the room which served as my bedroom until we moved into suburbia overlooked a pawnbroker and a pub. *A Point of View* is set in that room: the action in fact hinges on the leading character's determination not to be evicted from the room. I could take anyone to the bridge over the canal where *Who's a Hero, Then?* takes place. During rehearsals of *The Birthday Party* (in which I played Petey with the author directing) Harold Pinter explained that the seedy boarding-house in which the action takes place was based on one he had known as an actor in seaside rep.

Or situations.... There was the visit with my mother to the hat department of a well-known store in the days before the ubiquitous check-out and when shop assistants assisted – if they could only be persuaded to break off their own absorbing conversation for long enough. That, with only the slightest exaggeration, became the sketch 'Service', which achieved a fair run in a West End revue. And anyone who has ever served on a committee will recognize the routine of *In Committee*.

Or people.... I knew a husband and wife exactly like those portrayed in *End of the Picnic*, though neither was any longer with us by the time I came to write the play: apart from avoiding the risk of a libel action, I would not wish to hurt anyone. Nor can the playwright ever draw a complete picture. A person is a person, a play a play, and the essence of writing is selection. In spite of points of resemblance to the actor-manager, Ronald Harwood insists that Sir in *The Dresser* is not Wolfit. In any case fiction must always be an imaginative reconstruction, a process in which change inevitably takes place. A case history belongs in a filing cabinet; a character has an independent life.

Other people's lives may touch off trains of thought, though. There are half a dozen stories in any edition of a newspaper. Only don't expect to find them among the headlines. Of course there is a feature film in an embassy siege or piratical seizure; but you can be sure that every big name in the business will have weighed up the topical potential too, and be negotiating a commission before you have finished the sports page. The real treasure is buried in those five or six-line stories filling up a column; incidents reporting explosions in otherwise ordinary lives. I remember one about a man apprehended for a minor misdemeanour, who rather meanly gave the police a friend's name and address instead of his own – not knowing the friend at that time was being sought by the force on a serious charge. I let that one go because coincidence at the centre of a story-line needs very careful handling. However I certainly used an article I read in a Sunday paper on the latest range of fall-out shelters. I was particularly struck by one *de luxe* model which came equipped with a twenty-year calendar, and wondered what anyone would be like after twenty years underground. Taking the situation a step further, I speculated on how children might grow up who had never seen the outside world. The result was *Little Brother, Little Sister*, which is still being performed years after those shelters have become redundant.

History might be regarded as being constructed from yesterday's newspapers. Just as one popular newspaper proclaims 'All human life' can be found in its pages, so the lives of countless millions like so many coral insects have gone to make the history books. History is all about people. For almost as long as theatre has existed plays have been written about historical characters. The great advantage they offer is that they come with their own stories attached. The disadvantage is that research is obligatory and can be time-consuming, while any findings must be used lightly. There is always a temptation to drag in laboriously quarried facts because they are on hand, whether or not they belong in that particular play. Sometimes facts can even be inconvenient. Did Shakespeare know that Richard III was the most libelled English monarch to date? Did he care? (He did an equally good, and almost as undeserved hatchet job on Macbeth, too.) He realized that a writer's first duty is towards the play. A play exists in its own right. For the melodrama Shakespeare had in mind it was essential that Richard be a Plantagenet monster, so a monster Richard became. (Quite apart from the fact that depicting Henry Tudor, the Queen's grandfather, as the unprincipled usurper he was, would not have been good for the health of any Elizabethan.) Shakespeare's portrayal of Joan of Arc was also biased. Shaw's play centuries later was intended to tell the truth about her. Arguably his masterpiece (written at the age of seventy, offering hope to all late starters) it still tells more about Shaw than it does about Joan. He uses her own words in the trial scene (towards which the play is structured) but even so the result is a work of fiction based on certain facts. The dramatist's laws are not the historian's laws. As long as this is kept in mind there is a store-house behind us that cannot be exhausted.

Literature offers an almost equally rich field of ready-made story-lines. Often a title carries its own selling point with it. With *Jane Eyre* in lights the theatre-goer tends not to search the small print for the name of the adapter. There is a risk that the story may be too well known, and issue taken with the treatment when favourite passages are cut or changed. This is inevitable. The structural demands of a novel or short story are not those of a play. On the most elementary level time scales need to be changed. Story-book lovers may gaze at each other in mute rapture for hours, but thirty seconds will be more than enough for most audiences. A novelist may write simply: 'They quarrelled', and pass on; while a playwright must include every exchange of that quarrel (or alternatively place it off-stage). Parts of a story tend to be told in dialogue when the dramatic tension has increased to a point where speech is essential (just as in a musical the characters will burst into song when words are not sufficient to convey their emotions). A play consists only of dialogue with bare stage directions. The best an adapter can hope for is to capture the tone of the original writer's voice. (This partly accounts for the number of bad adaptations of Dickens: he could write splendidly theatrical dialogue but his style is at its best in descriptions and asides, which are not so easy to incorporate.) In the first draft of an adaptation I made of Le Fanu's *Carmilla* I included as much of the original dialogue as I could, only to have the actresses object. The Victorian dialogue too obviously stressed the lesbian relationship, not to be spoken in public even in these enlightened days.

When making an adaptation it is advisable to put the story aside for some time after reading it and then make a synopsis of what is remembered. An old piece of Hollywood advice is not to read it at all in the first place, but to persuade someone else to do that and then tell you the story. In this way inessentials take second place and the outline stands out. Then go back to the original for details, though you may now find these need to be used in different ways and places. The way *not* to do it is to take scissors and paste to a book.

Adaptations are not an easy option. They can entail even more work than an original idea. The material takes just as much manipulation as is needed to present any subject in dramatic form; then in addition there is all the reading and research to be done on the book in question. (In spite of which the radio and television rates of payments for adaptations are only a percentage of those for original plays.) The result has to be judged on its own merits as a play, while offending as little as possible those purists who miss their favourite passages.

Some classics are so well known that we tend to forget that they had to be written down in the first place. The creations overshadow their creators. It is surely poetic justice that Mary Shelley's Frankenstein should be one of these, along with Defoe's Robinson Crusoe, Swift's Gulliver, and even Stoker's Dracula. These authors struck notes that raised echoes in our tribal consciousness, becoming part of our race memory. Was there really a time before Gulliver existed? Surely Dracula has always been with us. We recognize them almost as old friends – even those of us who have never read the printed word that first brought them to life.

We recall them as well as we remember other stories – stories that were in circulation even before printing was invented. These are more than mere tales – *Jack and the Beanstalk*, with its giant outwitted, *The Sleeping Beauty* and the awakening power of a kiss, *The Three Wishes* or how to make the worst of gifts – they contain universally accepted psychological truths. Moreover these stories are common to the entire human race, turning up again and again in different guises all over the world from the Indians and Inuit of America to the English countryside and the Australian outback. Every civilization has its own version of The Deluge. Every one of us carries such a store of basic plots in these legends and fairy tales that nobody should ever be at a loss for a story line. Didn't Cecil B. de Mille hold that it should be possible to make a film of any six pages of The Bible?

The Greeks who were the first playwrights used their own myths for their plays. Indeed the need to represent the gods to audiences was the reason for having the plays in the first place. Writers have turned to the Greeks for inspiration again and again. Giraudoux called his play *Amphitrion 38* because he calculated there had been thirty-seven other versions before that one. The hero of Euripides' *Hippolytus* is killed by a lie, falsely accused of making advances to his stepmother, Phaedra, who herself had fallen in love with him. This was the way in which the goddess Aphrodite took her revenge because the young man preferred horses to girls. (Though his parents must have really been to blame for giving him the name that he was only trying to live up to.) Racine later elevated the love-tormented woman to be the leading character of *his* play *Phèdre*. And a long way behind either of them, I used the same situation for a comedy, *Cock and Bull Story*. I mention this not to boast (although my comedy played to capacity throughout its first repertory run, no other producer could be persuaded to take it) but to show how a basic pattern can be used, changing character details and backgrounds to produce something entirely new.

This process can be applied to any outline. Try it in the early planning stage if inspiration dries up and/or the characters refuse to co-operate. A writer is in the god-like position of being able to change anything with a few strokes of the pen. Have you set your action in a suburban kitchen in Penge? Why not experiment with transferring it to a hotel foyer in Birmingham – or Berlin or even Bali? Your leading man works in an office? What difference would it make if he were a dustman or a test pilot or a jobbing gardener?

Logic will be required later in the process of construction: because 'this' happens then 'that' will probably follow. At this point though consider what difference to 'that' a changed 'this' would make. Right now the flow and variety of ideas are what count. Imagination will never be quite as unfettered again. Feel free.

There is magic in the words 'if' and 'suppose'. They are used all the time in daydreaming. 'If' and 'suppose' can change any situation from the dull and ordinary to the bizarre, the romantic, the comic, the terrifying.

A character in one of Scott Fitzgerald's Pat Hobby

stories discovered the way to write a screenplay is to 'get behind a camera and dream'. Dreams are subject to constant change – an armchair can become a hot-air balloon; the bank floor is carpeted with leaves; and nobody is surprised when the Queen of Sheba, who has come to unblock the drains, drives off in an ice-cream van. This is the dreaming mind taking the image it needs at any given moment.

The universe and eternity are the fields in which your imagination can play: habit and an arbitrary conception of what is usually done try to tie it down. In my time I have been asked to judge many playwriting competitions. I found almost invariably that most of the entries were set in suburban homes in the present day, with the predictable situations arising from that background. (I suppose because most entrants enjoyed a permanent diet of that sort of play.) Almost all submissions were competently written (the impossibly bad play came as a welcome relief) but they were as alike as the end products of a plastics factory. If only writers would be prepared to juggle with time and space, to examine the effect of different backcloths.

This sameness is also a complaint of script readers in the commercial theatre. Although eighty per cent of the scripts offered follow all the rules, are literate and even typed in the correct format, they are almost indistinguishable one from another. If questioned, the writers would probably say, 'But that is exactly like the show we saw last night'. True: but if the planners want yet another domestic comedy, they have their regular suppliers – the names that have delivered the goods in the past. If an unknown wants to be considered among the high-powered competition, that newcomer must be offering something the others have not got.

For further practical examination of the way in which playwrights have built on existing work compare *Alcestis* by Euripides with T.S. Eliot's *The Cocktail Party*. The resemblance may not be immediately apparent, but Eliot assures us that the one was based on the other. For his *The Elder Statesman* he used *Oedipus at Colonus* and for *The Family Reunion* the *Eumenides* of Aeschylus. This play is the last of the Oresteian trilogy which Sartre also used for *Les Mouches* and served Eugene O'Neill as a model for *Mourning Becomes Electra*. It is of interest to note that although O'Neill intended to write a 'Modern psychological drama using one of the old legend plots of Greek tragedy for its basic theme' he was originally undecided between the stories of Electra and Medea. Options were kept open while he made notes and balanced alternatives. The time elapsing between making that first note in his diary and the opening night of the play was five years, in all of which time writing and rewriting were going on, experiments being tried, rejected and accepted.

Drama is not all Greek tragedy, though. Perhaps the most used plot is *Cinderella*. Not only is this our most popular pantomime, but its combination of wish-fulfilment with the 'boy meets girl; boy loses girl; boy gets girl' formula has proved a lifeline for many a desperate hack. On a higher plane traces of the rags-to-riches theme can be detected (unconsciously no doubt) in stories as varied as *The Count of Monte Cristo* (with the Abbé Faria playing Fairy Godmother) and *Pygmalion* (Professor Henry Higgins doing the same for Eliza Doolittle).

With a little thought a way may be devised of adapting a reconstruction technique to general use. Take any play or story. Better make it one of the best because there is no point in starting with second-rate material. Moreover it should be a story to which you are attracted – there is even less point in spending valuable time on something you do not care for. Reduce the situation to its absolutely basic elements. Take away the names of the characters together with their appearance, background, or even gender. Label them merely A, B, C, D etc. like the characters in an old problem in arithmetic. Keep stripping away until nothing is left but the bare bones of their function in the story. For example *Twelfth Night* would come down to: Viola is in love with Orsino, who is in love with Olivia, who is in love with Viola. A neat circle. Because this is a comedy Shakespeare gives Viola an identical (if biologically improbable) twin, Sebastian; so the outline becomes A (mark I) loves B, who loves C, who loves A (mark II), in which case A (mark I) can be paired with B, and A (mark

II) with C to provide a happy ending.

Now rebuild on that foundation.... put it in the present. Make A a lesbian who desires B, a nymphomaniac who lusts after C, who is a masochistic coward and must have the support of the strong-willed A. Which is now the basic situation of *Huis Clos*. This does not mean that Sartre arrived at his situation by stripping down and rebuilding *Twelfth Night*, but merely demonstrates how very different plays can be related to the same base, and what effect the exercise of selection and variation can have.

Is there a mutter in the background of plagiarism, of complaint about writers who take the ideas of others without a by-your-leave or a thank you? This seldom happens consciously. If you are acquainted with a play or story, then you know what not to put in your own to avoid comparison. If you should read a story in which a dealer in stolen goods, who trains boys to pick pockets, is reformed by the visitation of three ghosts on Christmas Eve, you would suspect, not that the author had read *Oliver Twist* and *A Christmas Carol*, but rather that he had *not*. Most plagiarism is unconscious. In any case the truer you are to your own experience and beliefs, the more you try to speak with your own voice, in short the more of yourself you put into your work, the less likely such an accusation is to be levelled.

Without wishing to appear narcissistic, I have sometimes found inspiration in my own plays. Not by repeating a success (one way of working I have always found impossible, and writhe when asked, 'Why don't you write a play like ...') but by taking up a small point from a previous piece. At one time three plays followed each other in quick succession. In *Where Have all the Ghosts Gone?* a drunken mother plays the piano. The actress in this part gave such a splendid performance that I made up my mind, even during rehearsals, that a piano should play a prominent part in the next play I wrote for her. So the leading character in *Angel Unwilling* is a piano teacher. Freedom of choice being what it is, the actress eventually elected to play the other main part, and did not touch the piano at all. However she presided over a party scene in which I included a character to whom people spoke, but

who never replied. This silent part came over so well that
in my following play, *Parcel*, the leading character does not
utter a word. I can look back on other such sequences,
connected with this or that group, and have always found
continuity a great help. What a pity groups tend to break
up and directors to move on.

As long ago as the fifties, when Stephen Joseph started
his theatre-in-the-round in Scarborough, he would be
continually throwing out suggestions like, 'write me a
play in which nobody can see the actors' faces' – which
resulted in *Then....* He was also a very good actor, but
experienced difficulty in learning lines. To accommodate
him I adapted *Frankenstein*, so that he could play The
Creature with no more than an occasional grunt. In the
very first amateur group with which I was associated, the
personalities of the members suggested characters for
future plays that were written for them.

One request to beware of is the one that begins, 'You
must write a play for us some time'. Whoever puts a
proposition in those terms is unlikely to know what they
really want. From hard experience I have learned that,
whatever you produce, it will not be quite what they are
looking for. Whereas even an apparently impossible
specification can act as a spur.

For instance a youth group requested a play. At our first
meeting I confessed to a totally blank mind and asked for
suggestions. What sort of play did they want? They were
quite definite about wanting a horror play in nineteenth-
century costume, but were prepared to agree with me
that, for a change, it should be Regency rather than Late
Victorian. Casting at first seemed to present some
problems as the obvious actor for the hero had difficulty in
learning lines (where had I heard that before? – but better
to know in advance) and another member of the cast had
been blind from birth. These difficulties were turned into
assets as they were built into the fabric of the play. The
young man, on account of social differences (the question
of whether he should be a soldier or a curate took some
time to decide, but finally we settled on the Church) was
kept off-stage as much as possible. To avoid any
suggestion of playing for sympathy, the blind boy was

cast as the villain (also blind). One of the girls wanted to be a sinister housekeeper. Another had ideas about the village simpleton.... After the first meeting I rounded out the tentative characters and brought them together in a rough outline, of which everyone had a copy to read. After this, ideas for possible developments came thick and fast: if they all been incorporated, the final script would have played for six hours. However I fitted together as many as I could. The cast was free to make any further suggestions, all of which were noted, and none was discarded without careful consideration, but the actual writing of the play was entirely my responsibility. This form of collaboration all worked very well, and the play has had many productions since. (Even though Samuel French rejected it, commenting that it read like a collaboration between Jane Austen and Dennis Wheatley. As that was what we had all been aiming for, I took this criticism as a compliment.)

I have found that a careful briefing on the available cast, budget limits, performing conditions, etc. does not act as the strait-jacket that might be expected. Rather the solving of such problems as are raised can provide a stimulus to the imagination.

When commissioned to write a play for the EMMA touring company I had a long discussion with the director, from which I learned that he liked the comedies of Plautus (with characters slipping in and out of disguises and nobody turning out to be what they seem) and could I combine that with a detective story? These requests formed an outline within which scenes grew. It so happened that for years there had been in my ideas file a character called Ragerbo, who murdered people for their clothes, and who was just waiting to be fitted into the right play.

Suppose you were presented with a cast, one of whom had just broken a leg and could only walk with crutches, one of whom could understand but not speak English, one who was beautiful but dim and one who was bright as a button but ninety years old.... Suppose your stage had a scaffold pole in the middle of it.... You would have no option but to incorporate those elements into your finished script. To start with, how would you account for the scaffold pole? What would it be doing there? How would the characters react to it? As these questions were asked, more would be raised and before you knew where you were a synopsis would be on its way to being constructed.

But the subject of construction comes later.

3 That is the Question

Why does anyone write a play? At the highest level of optimism in the hope of fame and fortune? As far as fame goes, ask even a regular theatre-goer for the names of living playwrights, and you will be lucky if he uses two hands to count them. This is in spite of hundreds of typewriters at present turning out material for the stage. Ask a non-theatre-goer, and the reply is likely to be 'Yer what?' So much for fame. As for making a fortune, the business is so risky that the chance of winning a first dividend on the football pools is much higher.

What then is the lowest reward a writer will be prepared to settle for? It cannot be financial because (like many others) I have been prepared to write for no payment at all. Is it just the pleasure of seeing one's work staged? That dream can turn into a nightmare with a disastrous production. At the very lowest level I can hope only (a) that there will be customers and (b) that they will stay until the end of my play. Any more – laughter (in the right places), applause, a small performing fee, even moderately good notices recognizing that the actors did not make it all up as they went along – is a bonus. My aim, and I suggest the common aspiration of all playwrights, is simply to hold an audience.

This in itself is quite a feat. How is it achieved? By attracting and then holding interest. Technical dexterity in the use of words either as poetry, rhetoric, or the stand-up comic's string of jokes can do this for a while. A lecture, even without jokes, illustrations or practical demonstrations will beguile an assembly of enthusiasts. Some bad propaganda plays have succeeded in preaching at length to the converted: people will sit enthralled for hours while their prejudices are being confirmed. However a theatre audience is usually a motley collection of human beings, which may well include right-wing astronomers and left-wing head-hunters, mixed in with shop assistants and retired army officers; and the attention of them all must be fixed on one play at the same time. So is there anything that interests all human beings? Yes. Human beings are interested in other human beings. Which is why a machine minder from the Midlands can be enthralled by the lives of a middle-class Russian family of many years ago, or a professor of mathematics in Cambridge gripped by the career of a Scottish murderer of even further back.

Which is another way of saying that plays must be about people. Not language or abstract ideas or spectacular scenery, but fellow creatures. Occasionally these may be disguised as animals as in *Toad of Toad Hall*, or normally inanimate objects as in some of David Wood's children's plays, or they may even be abstractions as in medieval morality plays. However for the purposes of drama, Mole and Badger, Pepper Pot and Tea Bag, Goods and Knowledge, take on the attributes of human beings. They are bound to, because they are played by human beings. Even when this process seems to have been reversed, as in cartoon films and puppet shows, it is the likeness of the non-humans to ourselves that enables us to empathize.

Empathy, according to my dictionaries, is 'mental identification with the character and experiences of another person' or 'imaginative or emotional projection of oneself into the object of contemplation'. It is the state of mind that causes us to shred our handkerchiefs and twine our legs into knots as the train rushes towards the heroine tied to the railway track. Everybody knows that state of mind, but many would-be playwrights fail to understand its implication. This is: because we identify with characters, characters make the play.

Well-drawn, understandable characters may even save a play that is otherwise not well constructed. Empathy carries us through. Shaw is a dangerous model (indeed a fatally attractive one to some beginners) often seeming to break every rule of construction. Yet note in one of his most abstract pieces, which is all debate – the 'Don Juan in Hell' interlude in *Man and Superman* – the four characters are not only clearly defined but, as each sets forth his or her argument, that point of view helps to define the character. Moreover each character has a particular problem – of which more later.

Most plays have a leading character. True, Chekhov wrote plays without star parts but, if you want to follow his example, you must write plays that are as good as Chekhov's. Moreover audiences have a way of elevating a character to a star position, even if the author neglected to do so. Because of the way *The Cherry Orchard* is constructed – each character has an attitude to the loss of the family fortune, which could be put right by the destruction of the orchard – all the characters are of equal importance in saying what Chekhov wants to say. Yet in many productions Madame Ranevsky appears to be the lead, not only because the part is usually played by a star actress, but on account of the character's charm. The audience cares about what happens to her.

In all the world's great drama, one creation in each play tends to stand out above all the others. The plays may have strong supporting casts of well-drawn characters, but there is no doubt as to who the play is about. Many titles signal this fact by consisting merely of the name: *Agamemnon, Hamlet, Major Barbara*; or their main attribute: *The Miser, The Father, The Daughter-in-Law*. Occasionally this top billing would seem to be shared, as in *Romeo and Juliet*, or *Antony and Cleopatra*, though even there the female half of the partnership tends to predominate.

In the theatre, where a moment can seem an hour, it is desirable that our companions for the time spent there should have some attributes to make it worth while. Excepting the occasional masochist, or possible saint, nobody wants to stay any longer than they have to in the company of someone they find utterly repulsive. Which means that leading characters must have some qualities we find attractive.

Protagonist – a word coming from the Greek and meaning 'the leading actor' – is a useful word in these days of equality between genders, because it can apply equally to both male and female. How to make a protagonist attractive? The most obvious way if it is a man is to make him handsome, or if it is a woman to make her beautiful. Sheer physical attraction will often be sufficient to engage an audience. Unfortunately the casting of performers with this quality is out of the control of the playwright: at best he has the occasional power of veto. His stage directions may call for a Venus and an Adonis, but in the last resort he will have to settle for what is available locally, particularly with a small drama group; even if this leaves him with a double-chinned Adonis and a Venus with a squint. Better add to the mere good looks something else with which we can all fall in love on the most basic level – such as the sweet nature of a Cinderella.

Such perfection of character is rare in a protagonist, if only because the very nature of drama seems to demand flaws – Hamlet's indecision or Othello's jealousy. Nora in *A Doll's House* is a liar and a forger, while Henry Higgins in *Pygmalion* is an egocentric bully: but both have charm. Charm is not easy to define ('an indefinable power of delighting' says my dictionary) but it is instantly recognizable when it is encountered. Even Dracula has charm, which adds to his menace. There is something bird-like about Nora, and something of the naughty boy in Higgins.

Sheer strength of character, the quality of determination, can also compel admiration. Rose in *Gypsy*, or Joan in *Saint Joan* are unstoppable. Each of these has an added attraction in that their ambition, at least on the surface, is for others.

Ambition, however, can be quite selfish. In such cases the more ruthless the protagonist, the more fascinated we become, perhaps measuring our own weaknesses against their juggernaut progress as they claw their way to the top. Richard III, Macbeth, the heroes of *Deathtrap* and *How to Succeed in Business*, even such criminals as Scarface or Sweeney Todd, are acceptable dramatically, and not merely because we know the writer will have devised some means of retribution for the last scene. (Very occasionally one of these villains literally gets away with murder, especially when the writer, scenting success, has a sequel in mind.) In each case though the villain/hero is more than merely nasty – there is a compensating trait, if only the courage to take risks and defy conventional morality. Macbeth has a streak of poetry (which makes it a difficult part for actors). Sweeney Todd's delight in his bloody business is infectious: as with his childhood counterpart, Mr Punch, the audience applauds as the bodies fall. A variation in the counting of bodies made Don Juan the hero of at least three classics. Richard III has self-awareness and a disarming willingness to admit his villainies. He also has a sense of humour. The ability to make us laugh can be a blackguard's saving grace. If you can think of no other way to make a repulsive person acceptable, put him into a comedy. This was Molière's way. Harpagon, the miser, and Tartuffe, the hypocrite, are funny.

These are all large-scale characters. They would be difficult to contain within a modern semi or maisonette. Though David Turner managed this with Fred Midway in *Semi-Detached* and Phillip King with Emma Hornet in *Sailor Beware* (both in the Molière tradition) the modern tendency – perhaps influenced by the size of a television screen – is to scale down.

Moreover in an age of mass production everybody is expected to be more or less like everybody else. Even if a few, in an attempt to look different, wear clown suits or paint themselves with woad, before long they are lost in a crowd of lookalikes. So at first glance a character may seem to have no outstanding attributes – until these are brought out by problems.

There is nothing like having to make a decision for revealing the sort of person you are. Even a refusal to make it can characterize: look at Hamlet. Confrontation with a problem can make even a nonentity interesting. A mild-mannered unknown caught up in a bank raid is swept into the headlines (in which case he has two problems for the price of one). Conversely, the most dynamic persons can appear bores when pursuing the even tenor of their ways. The spectacle of them cutting a lawn or snoozing contentedly in a deck chair is totally undramatic, even if yesterday they should have crossed the Channel on a bedstead or have undivulged plans to steal the Crown Jewels tomorrow. If, however, a rifle with a telescope sight were trained on the lawn-cutter, or a bomb were ticking under the deck chair, interest would be aroused. We would start to wonder what was going to happen to those people.

Drama comes out whenever a question mark is written in. When an audience begins to worry about what is to become of a character, then you are on your way to hooking them.

To stay for a moment with that bomb under the deck chair.... The speculation aroused by a threat to a total stranger (as long as you yourself were at a safe distance) would at best be disinterested. If, however, the snoozer were your Uncle Fred, then you would become involved. You might want to shout a warning, to dash to the rescue or at least to await the outcome with fingers in your ears. But you would not be indifferent. Knowing the character brings you into the action.

On the other hand suppose the character is not asleep, but bound and gagged, knowing very well that the bomb is due to go off at any time. (Equally suppose that there is nothing you can do to help, which is always your position in the audience.) The character can just lie there and let the explosion happen, which tells you something about him (and raises the question of *why* he did nothing); or he can struggle, either to shake off his bonds or to escape from the deck chair. Will he manage it in time? The fact that you are asking means that your interest is engaged. And the way in which he has reacted to the problem has characterized him.

Although there is no necessity for the disturbing influence to be so lethal, even in the lightest-weight farce it should *seem* a matter of life and death. Kenneth Tynan said that great drama was always about a man at the end of his tether. This can be as true of Charley's pseudo-aunt as it is of Oedipus. To most of us a spot on the nose is a mere inconvenience: to a young actress going for a screen test it *could* be a matter of life and death. A man facing a firing squad is not greatly worried by a spot on the nose: the spotty girl might *prefer* a firing squad.

So, just as their reactions to problems define characters,

the questions raised are as various as the characters themselves. In a way the characters create their own particular problems. There is nothing like falling in love for unsettling one's future. The boy-meets-girl situation has been a mainstay of drama since time immemorial, but how differently Falstaff, John Worthing, Romeo and The Phantom of the Opera deal with it. Losing your job can be a mild inconvenience to a Billy Liar or a fatal blow to Willy Loman or Marie Antoinette. Even coming into a fortune can create problems, as Kipps and Pip from *Great Expectations* discover.

Perhaps the easiest way of raising a question mark is to make the leading character want something. Cinderella wants to go to the ball. Richard III and Macbeth want to become king (and thereafter to stay king). Oedipus wants to find out who is responsible for bringing the plague to Thebes. Higgins wants to pass off a flower girl as a duchess. Lord Fancourt Babberley wants to pass himself off as Charley's aunt. Barrie's *Dear Brutus* is apparently a play without a central character; instead it is made up of a number of mini dramas in which the characters all want the same thing – a second chance. (Though any writer attempting as complex a piece of play construction as *Dear Brutus* had better be as assured a theatre technician as Barrie.) Once we identify the protagonist's desires, we become involved in the actions. This happens even in Brecht's plays. Grusha, in *The Caucasian Chalk Circle*, wants to keep the child. In the audience we too want her to keep it, so we stay with the play to find out whether we shall all get what we want. To save time and paper, let us call 'the thing that is wanted' by the more technical term of 'the objective'.

Sometimes we do *not* want the protagonist to achieve that objective. We do not want the villain in *Dial M for Murder* to succeed in his ingenious plan to kill his wife. The playwright villain in *Deathtrap seems* to succeed, but thereafter we wait to see whether he will get away with it. (Being a commercial melodrama we know that he won't, but the fun lies in seeing exactly how he comes unstuck.) We do not want the vampires Dracula and Carmilla to kill the heroine, and the nearer they come to success the greater the dramatic tension. We do *not* want the gangster Arturo Ui (Brecht again) to take over the district. In this instance he succeeds, pointing up Brecht's message that we should all have done more to stop the rise of Hitler.

Sometimes an outside force threatens the protagonist. The question then becomes 'How to escape?' This is not as negative as it may at first seem. If someone points a gun at you, you positively want to stop him from pulling the trigger. The objective here is to prevent something from happening. Take two of my own plays.... In *Point of View* Auntie wants to avoid being evicted from her room with a view. In *Usher* Roderick wants to prevent his sister Madeline's marriage. In both cases the protagonist succeeds, though Roderick Usher does so in a way he had not expected. In Ibsen's *A Doll's House* Nora wants to prevent her husband from finding out about her forgery; or looked at the other way she wants to preserve the domestic harmony that prevailed before the blackmailer arrived.

So sometimes the objective is to maintain the *status quo*, to keep the way of life what it has always been. This is what the family in *The Cherry Orchard* deeply wants, even though it cannot be done without putting back the clock – which is impossible. So they seem to flounder helplessly while the worst comes to the worst. However Chekhov raises a question mark by seeming to offer a lifeline. Will they take it? In the end they cannot, because it would mean changing the conditioning of a lifetime. *Mother Courage* just wants to go on trading, living off the war which will eventually destroy her. She likewise cannot change her way of life.

In those two cases there is an added dimension. Although the audience can see what is threatening, the characters can not. This is similar to the much cruder version of the bomb under the deck chair. Our sympathies and fears for the future of people can be aroused even though they themselves are blind to impending disaster. In *Night Must Fall* we suspect that the amiable young man has killed once and could kill again. We know that Beidermann's lodgers in *The Fire Raisers* are arsonists. The big question is can the almost inevitable catastrophe be averted?

Sometimes a decision has to be made by the protagonist, as in Ibsen's *Lady from the Sea*. Shaw's *Candida* has to decide between the poet Marchbanks and her husband. In *The Doctor's Dilemma* Colenso Ridgeon has to decide who shall be treated for tuberculosis (then a killing disease) – the dull but worthy doctor or the brilliant but immoral painter. In such plays the cases for and against must be clearly presented. As in a tug of war, the greater the pull on each side, the greater the tension. The more difficult the decision, the more powerful the drama.

Just as great drama is about persons stretched to their limits, so the higher the stakes, the greater the potential interest. Nora does not face temporary embarrassment, but the break-up of her marriage. In *Night Must Fall*, if Danny were merely a small-time thief, we would not hold our breath as we do when we know that he is a psychopathic murderer. Sir Thomas More in a *A Man For All Seasons* knows that his life depends on winning the legal argument with Henry VIII. The lives of others may be involved with that of the protagonist. The future of entire states hangs on the loves of Antony and Cleopatra – or the decision of the king in *Crown Matrimonial*, the probing of Oedipus, the murder of Agamemnon or the revenge of Electra.

In spy-thriller melodramas the very fate of the world frequently hangs in the balance. These, in spite of the highest stakes, are not high dramas, because we know in advance that the hero will succeed – that is part of the contract with the audience. For a similar reason my play, *The Laboratory*, is a comedy. Although Gabriotto (the apothecary accused of selling poison) faces execution unless he can prove his innocence, the flawed characters opposing him are so frivolous and corruptible that his task is made easier.

It might be said that the size of the question mark categorizes the type of play. A big problem engenders tense drama. A small problem – say of who should marry whom – produces a comedy. A tiny problem – such as who is pretending to be whom – results in farce. The difference between these types of play does not lie in the surface dialogue (the tragedy of *Hamlet* is full of witty lines, even jokes) but in the issues at the very core. Consideration of this aspect of the basic idea in the early stages of planning a play can avoid much rewriting later on. Farces have failed because the initial premise was too serious for the audience to accept trivially and, for the opposite reason, audiences have exploded with laughter at situations the author intended to be taken seriously.

However there can be no question mark at all if the problem is too easily solved. As a simple example set a scene in a shop. You ask for a bar of chocolate, pay for it, the shopkeeper hands it over and you leave with the chocolate you wanted. No drama at all. But suppose the shopkeeper tells you that the brand of chocolate you want is out of stock. Then you have to make a choice – either to make no purchase or to select something else from the range of goods. Or suppose, as you are about to enter, you see a dog standing in the doorway, and you have to pass it to go in. Moreover it looks very large and fierce. If you want to buy your chocolate, you must first placate the dog. But then suppose, unseen by you, there is a gunman behind the door making threatening gestures to the shopkeeper: the shopkeeper grimaces at you, but you cannot understand those facial signals – will you be warned in time? None of this is world-shattering drama, but the beginnings of a dramatic situation are recognizable. Each of those suggestion-raising situations prevents your getting the chocolate you want. Each represents an obstacle. An obstacle is an indispensable element in the question.

See how it applies to some of the examples already quoted. Higgins wants to pass off Eliza as a duchess, but he can't because she talks and behaves like a flower girl. Cinderella wants to go to the ball, but can't because she has nothing to go in. Roderick Usher wants to keep his sister from marrying, but can't because her lover intends to take her away. The Ranevsky family want to live in the way they have always done, but they cannot keep up with changing times. The characters in *Dear Brutus* want a second chance, but their own natures will always lead them to repeat their mistakes. James Bond is always up against SMERSH, SMASH, SPLASH or the sinister agency of whatever foreign power is currently reviewed with disfavour.

Here then are the elements that go to make any dramatic situation; that are bound to raise questions about the future of the people in the play. There must be someone who wants something, and something is stopping them from getting it. Ferdinand Brunetière defined this as: 'The spectacle of a will striving towards a goal, and conscious of the means which it employs'. That may sound rather like the wording of an official set of Civil Service rules, but the basic idea is one that every major playwright seems to have been born knowing. More is needed to achieve success: a knack with words, a feeling for the current climate of opinion, and understanding of what the public wants – or at least will be prepared to accept; but Brunetière's 'Law of the Drama' is there to build on. At some time during my early doodlings, when I am tinkering with the idea for a new play, I nearly always find myself asking, 'Who is this play about?' 'What do they want?' 'What is stopping them from getting it?'

Once aware of those elements you can begin to manipulate them. The dog in the sweet shop can be anything from a corgi to a wolfhound. It may respond to flattery, or bribes or a kick. It may respond to your advances by running away, licking your face or sinking its teeth into your ankle. You may be seeking, not a bar of chocolate, but the plans of the NATO defences. The principle remains the same.

Nor is the obstacle overcome at a single blow. Otherwise the play will be very short. Take another simple scenario....

You settle down to enjoy your tea – scones with raspberry jam. A fly is also attracted to the jam and comes buzzing around your head. You wave it off with your hand. Then you realize it is no ordinary fly, but a striped one with a sting at the end. What is more, it resents hands being waved at it and responds by diving at you. Believing attack to be the best form of defence, you roll up a newspaper and take a swipe at the wasp. But miss. The wasp is now determined to put you in your place. A duel develops. You have weight on your side, while the wasp has speed and manoeuvrability on its side. The encounter will end either with a flattened insect or a dash for the medicine chest.

That miniature drama contains all the elements. At first harmony reigns. That harmony is disrupted. A struggle ensues. Finally harmony is restored, though the initial situation will have been changed: in that mini-drama either you will continue your tea in some discomfort or the world will have one wasp fewer.

In a play of mine, *Boo!*, a little boy describes in the working of a bear trap the means by which he brings about the downfall of the play's leading character.

> You need a log of wood and a tree. Oh, and a pot of honey, because bears like honey, you see. Well, you tie the log to the branch of a tree so it hangs down, and you put the pot of honey underneath. Well, along comes the bear and sees the honey, because bears like honey, but it can't eat the honey because the log is in the way, you see. So it pushes the log out of the way. Well, the log swings back and hits the bear. The bear doesn't like being hit, so he hits the log. Well, back comes the log even harder. And the bear gets really angry and really hits the log. Well, the log goes up right out of sight, and the bear thinks now it can sit down and eat the honey. But while the bear isn't looking, down comes the log again, and – boom! The bear falls down. It's quite easy really.

Understanding that much, the boy could have gone on to become a successful playwright, because he was describing the interaction of protagonist, objective and obstacle.

An obstacle can be a thing, a state of mind, a social climate, a state of affairs.... Often it has to be personified. Although Romeo and Juliet are kept apart by the feud between their families, it is Tybalt, acting as a Capulet, who provokes the brawl in which he is killed and which causes Romeo's banishment. Though the obstacle *can* be a person in their own right, such as the conventional villain in an old burlesque melodrama. When the obstacle is a person, the more evenly matched that character and the protagonist, the more bitter will be the conflict and the more tense the development.

I have until this point deliberately avoided using the word 'conflict' because, although it can be found in most dramatic situations, there are times when it is very difficult to define. Where is the conflict in the *Night Must Fall* situation? There is a threat in the gradual revelation of

Danny's character, and some of the other characters dislike him, but not to the extent that could be called conflict. The tension here is derived from the uncertainty – will he or won't he? This also applies to the type of thriller in which the characters drop off one by one, such as Agatha Christie's *And Then There Were None*. There we wait to see who will be the next to go and speculate on the survival of the hero. He wants to stay alive, but it is of the essence of the well-worn plot that we do not know who is responsible for the mayhem. In Maeterlinck's play, *The Blind*, a group of blind people are lost in a forest and their leader, who was sighted, is dead. They do not realize that he is dead, but wait for him to lead them on. That raises a major speculation as to their future, but who is in conflict with whom?

It is perhaps easier in early plays for a writer to create opposition in a person than in a state of affairs. Two people can meet face to face and thrash out their differences. Society or social conditions or the class structure make intangible enemies (unless represented by other characters) and the audience may come to feel that your protagonist is making a lot of fuss about nothing. Jimmy Porter in *Look Back in Anger* is protesting about the world into which he was born, in which 'there aren't any good brave causes left', but he can't vent his frustration on the uncaring world, so he turns it on his wife – which many critics of the first production thought unfair. On the other hand, in *The Caretaker* Davis wants to move into the flat, but Mick is determined to have him out – a simple, easily understood base to which overtones, implications and atmosphere of unease are added.

Even here, though, a cautionary note should be sounded. It is possible to create a secondary character who diverts the interest of the audience away from the main character. It might be called the Iago syndrome. Shakespeare obviously intends Othello to be his prota-gonist, because that is the title of the play; yet without good direction and a very strong Othello, Iago captures the attention. This is because all the volition comes from Iago. He tells us what he wants to do – to ruin Othello – and, however imperfectly motivated, we can watch him putting that plan into effect. He acts while Othello is acted upon. Our sympathies are with Othello – his position is that of the unsuspecting heroine with the villain creeping up behind her: we want to shout, 'Look out!' – but it is Iago who carries the play forward.

The dramatic situation applies not only to the overall structure of a play, but also to scenes within it. Or even to tiny sections within scenes as the plot-line develops from one point to the next. If a scene sticks in the writing, or insists on taking a wrong direction, ask who at this point (not necessarily the leading character in the play) wants what and what is stopping them from getting it. You may as well be prepared because, when a play gets into rehearsal, the actors will start to mutter about motivation, which is another way of saying, 'What do I want?'

Not every scene in a play need be dramatic – though it should contribute to the overall dramatic structure (and if it does not, its presence should be queried). A scene can be purely lyrical as when Enobarbus describes Cleopatra's barge, or Lorenzo and Jessica listen to music in the moonlight, or – exercising verbal dexterity in a different way – the scandal-mongers in *The School for Scandal*. A scene may be used to establish atmosphere as does the witches' scene at the opening of *Macbeth*, or the card game at the beginning of *The Odd Couple*. The purpose of these scenes is to put the audience in the right frame of mind for what is to follow. A scene may be used to convey to an audience information that will be necessary to their understanding of what follows. Prospero telling Miranda how they came to be marooned on the island at the beginning of *The Tempest* or Helen's parents at the beginning of *The Miracle Worker*, learning of her handicaps. Usually even an expository scene serves more than one purpose: the opening scene of *Usher* in which Madeline is shown to be mentally ill is both expository and atmospheric; the opening of *The Caretaker* with Aston showing Davies round the room, sets the scene and also explains how the two men came to be there. These scenes, although containing no dramatic clashes, contribute by foreshadowing the question mark which is to develop. In particular an opening scene can show the *status quo*, the state of harmony that is to be disturbed.

If you can understand the principles behind creating that question mark, you should have no difficulty in developing your original idea into the basic outline for a play. There is a lot more work to be done yet, but at least you will have made a start.

4 Nuts, Bolts and Hinges

I quite agree: when you have wound a clean sheet of paper into your typewriter and your fingers are poised above the keys, it is irritating to have anyone shout 'Stop' or 'Think'. I hate interruptions, too; though personally speaking at this stage for me the tool in question is not a typewriter but a stub of old pencil, to be used in conjunction with a pile of scrap paper or even the backs of used envelopes. There is a reason for this besides my naturally penny-pinching nature. A page of typescript looks so neat that only the really flint-hearted can be expected to bring themselves to make alterations all over it. Yet that is almost certainly what will be demanded before the final draft. There is such a temptation to murmur, 'Yes, I know I ought to cut that half-dozen speeches, but if I do, I'll have to retype the whole scene – so let it pass.' If there is no doubt about having to retype anyway, you can feel free to slash with abandon. An exception may perhaps be made for those whose handwriting is so bad that even they themselves have difficulty in reading back; but they are advised to type their first draft on paper that cannot be shown to anyone else. (At this point a lively debate could spring up as to the pros and cons of word processors, but this is neither the time nor place to be drawn into it.)

The more thought that goes into a play at this stage, the fewer alterations that will need to be made later. Hence the 'Stop' and 'Think'. Try to hold back on dialogue (wherein lies most of the fun of writing) until you are satisfied that the *shape* of the play is right.

By now you will have assembled your basic material. You think you know who the play is to be about. You have a nodding acquaintance with some of the characters; perhaps you know them as well as you do the people you travel to work with – and you will come to know them better: if all works out the way it should, they will even surprise you. You know something about their background: either it is one with which you are familiar or you will already have done some research. To some extent you know what you want to say. (Though again you may be in for a surprise. You may discover that you have said something you had not set out to say at all. Writing can be very revealing.)

The meaning of a play is contained in the arrangement of the material.

At this point you may object that you have never set out to write a play with a message, and do not intend to start; rightly protesting that enough bad propaganda plays have already been staged without your adding to their number. I am not talking about propaganda or messages but of meaning: and your play will have a meaning whether you like it or not. Almost any play becomes a form of parable.

Even the frothiest farce with nubile young ladies in varying stages of exposure, making ingenious use of the manifold exits and entrances provided by an experienced set designer, will carry a meaning. This could be that you can carry on whatever extra-marital activities you please as long as the wife does not find out; or it may be that, cover up as assiduously as you like, the wife inevitably *will* find out. If at the offset you as a writer know what you are trying to do, there is less chance of discovering at the end that you have done something you did not intend.

To call this implicit meaning 'the theme' of a play can be misleading. Worse, it can lead to writers hunting for a tag to put on their wares and then constructing a play to fit; which is incongruous as designing a label and then making a garment to suit it.

Yet every writer is bound to have an attitude towards the material. We all have likes and dislikes. However apolitical or non-believing we may be, we know what we approve or disapprove of, if only of cats or cabbage. That is all part of being an individual.

As an example, Shakespeare seems to have had a

decided attitude towards revenge. In *Titus Andronicus* revenge breeds revenge. *Hamlet* hinges on revenge: if the Ghost had not insisted on being revenged the action would never have begun, and if Laertes had not insisted on being revenged for the deaths of his father and sister, it would not have been wound up in the way that it was. You can argue that this was merely the formula of the revenge tragedy popular at the time, revenge being as good a way as any of achieving an impressive pile of corpses in the closing scene; but revenge occurs in the comedies too. Shylock comes to grief, not because he is a Jew and a moneylender, which are merely factors providing motive and opportunity, but because he insists on pressing his revenge against Antonio. Forgiveness is the reverse of revenge. At the end of *Measure For Measure* the monstrous Angelo is forgiven. *The Tempest* is about a man who has the power to exact revenge, and reasons enough for doing so, but prefers to forgive. The author's attitude shows.

A playwright's meaning is conveyed by what he displays to the audience, by selecting and arranging.

What characters are seen to do matters more than what they say. In fact what they say can be in complete contrast to what they are doing; as for instance the stock thriller situation with the villain making love to the heroine whom we know he is planning to murder. In Coward's *Present Laughter* a couple make love while comparing the acoustics of the Albert and Queen's Halls. Facility with dialogue does not necessarily make a good playwright. Pages of slick speeches may provide an entertaining first reading, but the play will fall apart on the stage if the structure underneath those speeches is not sound.

A play has to be written in the third person (that is, from the point of view of the audience) because a playwright cannot interpose himself between the action and the audience in the way that a novelist can. When he tries – as for instance in the use of a narrator – the device is seldom successful. It seems to work in Thornton Wilder's *Our Town*, but the meaning of that play would come over even if the narrating Stage Manager were taken out, because the theme is contained in the action; particularly Emily's return to one day in her life, discovering how little the living make of what they have. Brecht is constantly signalling his intentions, sometimes with placards, captions and projections; but I believe he underestimates the intelligence of the audience and his own dramatic powers. We see how war takes the children of Mother Courage away from her one by one at the same time as we are shown how she persists in scraping a living around the soldiers' camps. What conclusion are we to draw from that? That war is profitable? In *The Caucasian Chalk Circle* we see Grusha risk everything she has, including her life, to protect a child that has been abandoned by its mother. When later in the play the question is raised as to who should keep the child, would anyone in the audience vote for the uncaring natural mother?

The ending of a play is particularly important, not only because that last scene is the one most likely to make an impression on the audience, but because it sums up all that has gone before. If at the end of *The Crucible* John Proctor had recanted and agreed to co-operate with the authorities, the meaning of the play would have been reversed. At the end of *Private Lives* Amanda and Eliot tiptoe away together – in spite of their constant fighting, they belong together. Shaw added the epilogue to *Saint Joan* because, as he pointed out, it was absurd to end with her burning and not her canonization. Similarly Anouilh in *The Lark* felt that the story had to end in triumph and so brings down the curtain on the crowning of the Dauphin. At the end of *Pygmalion* Shaw found his play saying something that he had not intended: it is all very well for the author to add a postscript telling us that Eliza married Freddy, but no audience believes him. The way the play has been constructed leaves Eliza and Higgins firmly paired.

Beware of the fake ending. That is the happy ending tacked on to placate a section of the public (and in the bad old days of the Lord Chamberlain, the censor) but which, if taken seriously, would cancel out everything that went before. Audiences are not happy at this, merely feeling cheated by death-bed repentance or last-minute reformation. We know that, for all his protestations, the rake of

Restoration Comedy will not turn from womanizing. In my *George Davenport, Highwayman*, the eponymous hero is quite prepared to make a speech at the gallows regretting his wicked ways – because he knows that no one will believe him. If there is to be a sudden twist, then it must be carefully prepared for.

This also applies to nick-of-time rescues and revelations by characters of whose existence until that point the audience has been kept in ignorance. If the cavalry is to save the day, we must at least have been warned that the cavalry was in the area. A favourite device of bad melodrama was the sudden appearance of a long-lost uncle from Australia who, having made a fortune in the gold-fields, could put any situation to rights. Greek drama used the device of the *deus ex machina* – the god who would come down and sort out an apparently insoluble problem; but the Greeks were used to the activities of the gods, who were never far away and frequently became involved in human affairs. The Greeks believed more devoutly in their gods than we do in that relation from overseas, or the chance discovery of a missing will, letter or birth certificate.

In expert hands the *deus ex machina* can be used effectively, if somewhat cynically. In *Tartuffe* the hypocritical villain is put down by the intervention of The King. At the end of *The Beggar's Opera* MacHeath is saved from the gallows by a reprieve (brought about by some hasty, last-minute rewriting on the part of the Beggar/author). But these remedies imply that, if they are all that can be hoped for, then there is really no hope at all.

There are four main ways of ending a play.

The protagonist gets what he wants and is happy. This is perhaps the most usual ending, because it sends the audience home also happy at the way events turned out.

The protagonist gets what he wants, but is *not* happy. Oedipus unmasks the villain, but discovers that he is the guilty man. In *The Little Foxes* Regina gets command of the fortune she wanted, but loses her daughter in the process. Hamlet avenges his father, but dies in the process.

The protagonist does not get what he wants and is unhappy. The family in *The Cherry Orchard* lose both the orchard and their home. Othello kills himself. Eddie Carbone in *A View from the Bridge* fails to prevent his niece's marriage to an illegal immigrant and is disgraced.

The protagonist does not get what he wants, but discovers compensations that make up for the disappointment. This is probably the second most usual ending. Frequently the protagonist realizes that his objective was not so desirable (or was even antisocial), renounces it, and rides off into the sunset with the heroine as a prize for making the right decision: a Hollywood routine for sugaring the pill.

It may be worth mentioning at this point that the end of the story-line need not necessarily be the end of the play. Certainly in melodramas, thrillers or other action-packed plays the story may not be over until the very last line: in *The Monkey's Paw*, 'I wish him dead and at peace'; in *The Drums of Oude*, 'The Highlanders are here and we are saved!' *Carmilla* ends with the destruction of the vampire. *Dial 'M' for Murder* ends with the returning footsteps which prove the villain's guilt as the curtain falls. However the nature of a play may call for the slow unwinding of tension. If a play ends with a return to stability, it may be desirable to show this new balance at some length.

Lopakhin reveals that he has bought the Ranevsky estate at the end of Act Three of *The Cherry Orchard*, thus ending all hopes of saving the orchard; but the whole of Act Four is taken up with the family's departure, a gentle decline to the silence at the very end, broken only by the sound of axes against trees. Shylock is thwarted at the end of Act Four of *The Merchant of Venice*, but there is still another act before the end of the play.

So there may be minor characters to be disposed of, and sub-plots to be tied up. The action may have raised other issues which cannot be left unsettled. After Eliza has been successfully passed off as royalty, the subsidiary question is raised of what is to be done with her.

Not every 't' needs to be crossed or every 'i' dotted – audiences have imagination and can work some things out for themselves – but they do object to being left without any clues at all. This seems to be a repeated fault with much current writing. I suspect the guilty parties here to be not so much writers as producers, who make the final decision as to what audiences will see. It may be that the question raised has no solution simpler than a complete change of the social system, but if such is the case, the writer must make that situation clear. The play should lead up to and make a special point of such a no-hope ending, just as Tartuffe's hypocrisy is shown to be unbeatable short of divine intervention.

The rest of the play is an articulated structure, the scaffolding which supports the playwright's intentions (if that is not a mixed metaphor and engineering improbability). This scaffolding can be assembled in any design known to man (and in some ways yet to be dreamed of) because the parts from which it is constructed are never quite the same from one play to another. This is true even of the most commercial thriller or situation comedy written to rigid formulae laid down in the producer's office. Those parts come in all shapes and sizes because they are selected from the whole range of human experience. Change just one part and you change the play.

However, although the choice of materials is infinite, the nuts and bolts are standard. There are only a few of them, but only a few are needed. And in most plays all are used. They have comfortingly common names.

AND. (Not to be confused with AND THEN – which is to play construction what a granny knot is to a reef, more of which later.) It may in fact also be called ALSO.

THEREFORE. In mathematics this is written $\therefore$. It can also be viewed the other way up $\because$ in which instance it is known as BECAUSE.

BUT. Which should be self-explanatory.

To elaborate on each....

AND is mainly used to lay the foundations of a play. The more ANDs there are in early notes, the more solid the foundation is likely to be. AND links the circumstances in which the action takes place, and fills in the background. To take some well-known plays....

Macbeth wins a decisive victory against rebels AND is promoted by the King AND witches promise that *he* will be king AND the King decides to stay the night with the MacBeths.

Or, in *Twelfth Night,* Orsino is in love with Olivia AND Viola is wrecked on the coast of Illyria AND for safety, Viola disguises herself as a boy AND takes a job at Orsino's court AND falls in love with Orsino.

Or, to take a rather more modern play, *What Every Woman Knows....* John Shand is a serious-minded young man, anxious to improve himself, AND the Wylie brothers have a bookcase full of books, which John needs for his studies and cannot afford AND the Wylies have a sister, Maggie, whom they would like to see married.

Any of the above ANDs could be replaced by ALSO, but note the difference between that and AND THEN. AND links together circumstances (Henry Higgins is a professor of phonetics AND Colonel Pickering has come to London to confer with him AND bets that he can not pass off Eliza as a duchess): AND THEN merely links a sequence of events in time.

Any simple children's story can be linked with a series of AND THENS. 'I went into the woods *and then* I met a rabbit *and then* I met a fox *and then* I talked to an owl *and then* I came home *and then* went to bed.' Any two incidents in sequence can be linked by AND THEN. 'I picked a cabbage in the garden *and then* I made an apple pie.' 'He listened to a comedy show on the radio *and then* he shot himself.' The incongruity of those statements stems from the assumption that the second event is linked to the first by cause and effect rather than by a mere sequence in time. Even in a picaresque novel where the hero bounces from scrape to scrape, one adventure begins because another has just ended – he takes a job as a barman because he has just lost one as a schoolteacher. More than a few examples of merely AND THEN in your outline, for which you cannot read ALSO, suggests that you have a meandering story-line that does not hold together dramatically. Make sure that every AND adds to the basic situation.

THEREFORE in an outline indicates a logical progression of events. Using the second of the building devices, an integrated plot-line can be developed from a clearly understood basic situation. THEREFORE is concerned with the reason why people behave the way they do.

Duncan stands between Macbeth and the crown THERE-FORE Macbeth murders him.

Orsino's messages to Olivia have no effect THEREFORE he sends Viola to plead for him.

Sometimes a plot can be devised backwards. We know where we want to end, but how do we get there? By asking 'why' and getting the answer 'because'. BECAUSE is THERE-FORE the other way up.

Othello murders Desdemona BECAUSE Iago has persuaded him that she has been unfaithful.

Tony in *Dial 'M' For Murder* lies to the police BECAUSE he wants his wife to be convicted of murder.

Lord Fancourt Babberley in *Charley's Aunt* impersonates an elderly lady BECAUSE his friends need a chaperone.

'Why' is a word the playwright is likely to hear frequently in preliminary discussions with a director and from the performers during the first days of rehearsal – even when the answer seems perfectly plain to the writer. Actors brought up according to Stanislavsky will demand reasons even for standing up, sitting down or crossing the room. This is called motivation. Unless the author has provided motives the actors will invent them, and their suggestions may not be what the author had in mind. This is one reason for having the writer present at this stage in the production of a new play. While points are being clarified for the cast (although *always* through the director) weaknesses that might baffle audiences are also revealed and can be dealt with.

The reason why – or THEREFORE – is the device which links sections of the story together. Think of it with AND as nuts and bolts.

BUT, using a similar analogy, can be considered as a hinge (or bracket) which changes the direction of a story-line. BUT is the factor which prevents the action being completed too early in the proceedings.

Macbeth murders Duncan, BUT Duncan's heir escapes.

Viola pleads Orsino's cause with Olivia BUT Olivia falls in

love with her.

Cinderella goes to the ball BUT forgets the time.

Lord Babs successfully passes himself off as a wealthy widow BUT is then pursued by fortune hunters.

Obviously the use of AND, BUT and THEREFORE will depend on the type of play. BUT, for instance, will be used more in a farce or melodrama than in light comedy or drama, in plays that depend more on action than on character development. However any play will need to use some of these devices at some time.

Just as it may be useful to test the dramatic validity of an *idea* by reducing it to no more than one paragraph or a few sentences, at this stage you may find some benefit in laying out the skeleton of the play on one page just to see how it hangs together. In this way you can make sure that one event really does lead to another; that the motivations behind a character's actions are strong enough; and indeed that there is enough material here for a play of the length you have in mind.

Even when adapting existing material this layout is a help, not only because it will outline the dramatic situation, but it will demonstrate where expansion, contraction or new invention may be needed.

As an example let us look at an outline of *The Mikado*. (Chosen not only because it is well known, but because the issues are clear and the characterization simple.)

The Mikado of Japan decrees that any man caught flirting shall be executed.

AND his son, Nanki-Poo, attracts the attentions of Katisha, an elderly court lady.

AND he is ordered to marry her – or else.

BUT Nanki-Poo has fallen in love with Yum-Yum.

THEREFORE he disguises himself as a wandering musician AND runs away to look for her.

BUT when he finds her in the town of Titipu he learns that she is to be married to Ko-Ko, the executioner.

THEREFORE he decides to commit suicide.

BUT the Mikado has discovered that there have been no executions in Titipu lately and orders one to take place forthwith.

THEREFORE Ko-Ko comes to an arrangement with

Nanki-Poo: if Nanki-Poo will agree to be executed in a month's time, he can be married to Yum-Yum until then.

BUT Katisha discovers where Nanki-Poo is

AND tries to disrupt the celebrations

BUT she is turned away by Yum-Yum's friends

AND the wedding preparations go ahead

BUT they are interrupted by the news that the Mikado is on his way to the town

AND he will want to be told that there has been an execution

BUT Ko-Ko, who was a tailor before he became an executioner, cannot bring himself to chop off Nanki-Poo's head

THEREFORE merely issues a certificate to say that the execution has been carried out

BUT when the Mikado arrives with Katisha they realize that Ko-Ko is claiming to have executed the heir-apparent

AND 'encompassing the death of the heir-apparent' carries a death penalty

THEREFORE Ko-Ko pleads with Nanki-Poo to put in an appearance to prove that he is still alive.

BUT Nanki-Poo refuses if that involves marrying Katisha

THEREFORE Ko-Ko propose to Katisha and is accepted

AND Nanki-Poo reappears, married to Yum-Yum.

AND the Mikado is persuaded that 'nothing could be more satisfactory'.

This process of construction, using background, motive and complications as nuts, bolts and hinges is not necessarily achieved at a sitting. Days, weeks or even months of beavering may be necessary before the subconscious turns up, if not exactly the right idea, at least a lead that can be developed further. Beware of impatience, though. To start writing with inadequate preparation can lead to trouble later, and probably wholesale reshaping; while once a correctly articulated framework has been assembled, subsequent problems can be referred to it. Even if you are the sort of writer who starts with 'Act One – Scene One' and no idea of what is to follow until the final curtain, once the play is complete on paper in its draft stage, making an outline like this can be a help in pinpointing possible weaknesses, and suggesting improvements.

You may argue that all of this sounds arbitrary and mechanical, that a play cannot be constructed like a Lego or Meccano model and should be allowed to grow naturally as a living thing. Nonetheless all living things grow according to natural laws. DNA is a mystery to me, but I understand that every one of us carries within us the blueprint of our own development. The apple trees I can see from my window have grown naturally; yet so far not one of them has produced plums or put out roots where branches should be. Many unsuccessful plays try to do just that, changing purpose and direction in the middle. Usually they have just been allowed to grow.

Some established writers are on record as finding a scenario an encumbrance. Personally I have no inhibitions about changing anything if I think of something better – but those changes are made with reference to the outline, so that I know what effect on the closing scenes a diversion in the first half may have. Some playwrights prefer to do all this planning in their heads (there is no record of Shakespeare ever having made notes on bits of paper – which was probably too expensive in those days anyway). For some writers constant practice will have reduced the task of construction to an almost automatic reaction – constant and conscious practice will improve any craft, from driving to throwing pots. Some even seem to have been born with a faculty for plotting, just as some children can make music without having been taught – though I think it advisable not to assume that one was a little Mozart.

I must confess that once or twice I have written a play without apparent previous planning, and the result has been successful. The Life and Death of Almost Everybody has been performed all over the world, and I started that with no more idea in my head than a sweeper at work on the stage of a theatre. BUT I must also admit that I had constructed thirty or more plays step by step before trusting myself to uncharted seas in this way. AND that I was quite conscious of using BUT, AND and THEREFORE as the writing progressed.

If you have come this far, you will have a picture of the play you intend to write. The next question must be – how to present it to the audience?

5   Getting The Picture

At this point the shape of the play as it will eventually appear on stage should be taking form. Both Oscar Wilde and Agatha Christie (at different times) are reported to have announced that their next play was now finished – all that remained to be done was to add the dialogue. Speaking personally I have found that the longer I spend on these planning stages, the easier the actual writing is likely to be.

This shaping is what many writers think of as the real process of construction because it involves deciding where the action on stage is to begin, where it is to end, how an audience is to be held between the two and how it is to be divided into units of time.

At the risk of stating what may seem to be obvious, but because some would-be playwrights seem to have failed to notice the obvious, I will start by pointing out that a conventional full-length stage play is divided into one or two major parts, usually called acts, which may be further divided into small units called scenes. Usually between the acts the lights on the stage go out and lights over the audience come on. (This is often a signal for a dash to the theatre bar or to an ice-cream seller, or for other pressing needs, especially if there are many children in the audience – and is the reason why the writer has to devise ways of making them want to come back to their seats after the interval.) A rising and falling curtain may also indicate the beginning and end of an act. (In most professional theatres safety regulations require a fire-proof curtain to be lowered, which usually happens in an interval.) Between scenes a curtain may be lowered and raised, or lights may be lowered and raised, to indicate the passage of time and/or to allow for changes in the setting. These, however, are only conventions. Sometimes scene changes are made in full view of the audience. Sometimes the curtain is down when the audience arrives, sometimes it is up with the stage revealed.

There was a time when a play might have been divided into four acts (some operas still are) which meant there would have been three intervals. These days such a play would be more likely to be presented as a two-act play, with an interval coming after the second of the original acts. There is evidence to suggest that Shakespeare's plays were originally played straight through with no breaks at all. When Stephen Joseph opened his theatre-in-the-round in Scarborough there were no intervals because, he argued, selling neither drinks nor ice-cream there was no need for them. His production of *Hamlet* (although cut) was performed straight through in two and a half hours – and nobody walked out.

Most conventions have been arrived at for practical reasons. Lowering the lights over the audience and increasing them on the actors not only helps the audience to concentrate on what is happening on-stage, but advises them when the performance is about to begin. That convention, though, has only been in use for just over a hundred years, and was introduced when candles as a means of lighting the theatre were replaced by such improvements in technology as gas and electricity. Before that other means were used to indicate the start of proceedings – such as loud bangs with a stick off-stage or an actor entering to deliver a prologue. It is possible that you may want the audience to realize only slowly that the play has begun – I have done this several times, particularly in *The Life and Death of Almost Everybody* – in which case a different convention is used. However it is as well to get to know what current conventions are before deciding to challenge them.

Until now we have been preoccupied with imaginary worlds peopled by fictional characters; but now we are becoming involved with the real world of technicians, managements, front-of-house staff, actors, directors, audiences, etc. Practical considerations begin to impinge on our fantasies.

An arrangement of acts and scenes will appear at the beginning of a script something like this:

Act One	Scene One	Deidre's bedroom. Saturday night.
	Scene Two	Mary's living-room. Next morning.
	Scene Three	The same. Two hours later.
Act Two	Scene One	Mary's living-room. A month later.
	Scene Two	The same. Later that night.
Act Three	Scene One	Deirdre's bedroom. Next morning.
	Scene Two	The same. An hour later.

The same information will appear under or opposite the cast list on the printed theatre programme to advise an audience where and when the action is taking place. (Though that information should also be contained within the text of the play itself as not all members of the audience will have read the programme.)

Setting out the sequence of scenes in this way can give the writer some inkling of the proportions of the play. There are no hard and fast rules, though personally I like to see a balance in the arrangement; for instance if possible avoiding having a first act with one scene and a second act with ten. For the practical reason that the stamina of the audience may be lower in the second half, a last act shorter than the first is not a bad idea. (Even so a very long first act followed by a very short second in a two-act play is also to be avoided if possible.) In a three-act play the usual arrangement is to catch the attention of the audience in the first act; put the 'meat' of the play in the second (as in a sandwich); and move rapidly to a pay-off in the third. Alexandre Dumas is reputed to have replied to his son after being asked how to write a play – 'First act clear; last act short; all acts interesting.' As his son went on to write the classic *Camille*, he seems to have taken Father's advice.

There have been occasional exceptions to this division of a play into acts. Sartre's *Huis Clos* for instance is played through without an interval, so appearing to be a one-act play: however its running time of ninety minutes puts it into the full-length category. As does Anouilh's *Antigone*. There have been others. This scrapping of the interval usually happens where it is important that as little as possible is allowed to break the concentration of the audience – but it calls for a high degree of theatrical expertise on the part of the writer.

The running time of the usual full-length play is between one and a half and two and a half hours. Proving that there are exceptions to every rule, Albee's *Who's Afraid of Virginia Woolf* has a first act of ninety minutes (longer than the total running length of Coward's *Private Lives* or *Fallen Angels*); Shaw's *Saint Joan* runs for three and a half hours; and O'Neill's *Mourning Becomes Electra* and *The Iceman Cometh* are so long they are often performed with an interval for a meal. Shaw's *Back to Methusalah* and Ayckbourn's *Revengers Comedies* have to be split between two performances. Less established playwrights are not advised to follow these examples if they hope to get their play staged commercially.

The running time for a one-act play is usually between twenty minutes and an hour; though between twenty-five and forty-five minutes is the ideal to aim at, if only because those limits are set down in the rules of many festivals in which one-act plays are entered.

A play with a running time of between sixty and ninety minutes faces problems. One solution would be to add a second play to make it into a double bill as Peter Shaffer did with *The Private Ear, The Public Eye*, Alan Bennett did with *Single Spies* and Terence Rattigan did with *Separate Tables* and *Harlequinade*. Otherwise the play would need either to be expanded or cut – preferably the latter: many plays can be improved by cutting, few by expanding.

Where is the play to begin? The opening scene of a play need not necessarily be at the same point as the beginning of the outline of the story. For instance *The Mikado* opens with the arrival of Nanki-Poo in Titipu, disguised as a minstrel. The misunderstanding with Katisha, his falling in love with Yum-Yum, her betrothal to Ko-Ko and Ko-Ko being made Lord High Executioner have all happened before this.

A dramatization of *Cinderella* could go right back to the first arrival of the stepmother and stepsisters, with Cinderella reduced to the status of a servant. Or the opening scene could be one in which the invitation to the ball is received. (Sondheim's musical *Into the Woods* starts at this point.) Or the action could start in the middle of the story, with the ball in progress, Cinderella's arrival and the Prince trying to find out who the beautiful stranger may be. Much would depend on the sort of play intended. The first instance might be presenting the story as social comment on the stresses brought about within a family by a second marriage. The last could be developed as a sort of romantic semi-Hitchcockian mystery – 'Who is she?' 'What is she doing here?' And then, 'Where did she go?'

The later in the story the curtain goes up the more the audience will need to be put in the picture about what has gone before. This is known as exposition (of which more later) and requires some skill to put over without seeming obvious. Returning to *Cinderella*, if the play were to start with Father's remarriage, very little explanation would be needed because all the story would come after that; but if it were to open with Cinderella at the ball, then it would be necessary to explain at least about the stepsisters' cruelty and the godmother's intervention.

An advantage of starting early in the story is that the action can begin immediately, without having to fill in a lot of background. Shakespeare and Brecht tend to do this. For instance *Romeo and Juliet* starts with a street brawl in which the Montagues and Capulets are seen at each other's throats (and Romeo has not yet even set eyes on Juliet). With the exception of a short scene which mainly serves another purpose (again of which more later) *Twelfth Night* starts with Viola being washed up on the shore of Illyria. *Macbeth* starts with Duncan deciding to promote Macbeth (who has not yet met the witches). *Antony and Cleopatra* ranges over time and place as the play follows the story of the lovers until their separate deaths; but when Dryden wrote *All For Love*, using the same story (and even some of the dialogue) a century later, he had all the action taking place on one day in one place and the leading characters ending dead side by side. Brecht's *The*

Caucasian Chalk Circle could have been written as a courtroom drama with the rival mothers contending for custody of the child and all the past introduced by way of the evidence; instead he shows the servant girl, Grusha, escaping with the abandoned child and follows all her attempts to protect it. He even shows how the judge at the trial came to be made a judge.

The advantage of starting as late as possible is that, being nearer to the climax, the play will start at a high point of interest. If Ibsen had been writing like Brecht he might have opened *A Doll's House* with Nora committing a forgery to protect her husband: in fact he chose to open it years later, just before Nora is confronted by a blackmailer. The action takes place over only a few days. This means that dramatic tension is introduced early in the play, but at the price of having to explain a great deal of what has happened in the past.

Choosing where to start is a major decision.

Opening scenes have a special importance. In them a contract is as it were made with audiences, telling them what to expect. If these expectations are not fulfilled, or something quite different is eventually offered, an audience can be very unforgiving – and the audience is the final judge of whether a play is a success or failure. Setting aside sheer inspiration, for which we must all give thanks when it strikes, the craft of playwriting in many ways is the craft of manipulating an audience – of getting them to believe what you want them to believe; to laugh and cry when you want them to laugh and cry – in other words to accept what you propose to offer.

First consider what *sort* of play it is to be. To list the four main categories (though they may be subdivided almost indefinitely) – is it to be tragedy, melodrama, farce or comedy? They are different sorts of play – melodrama is not a cruder form of tragedy – the characters in *Death of a Salesman* live in different world from the characters in *Dial 'M' for Murder*. Nor is a farce merely a comedy with more laughs – even at first glance *No Sex Please We're British* will be seen to be a different sort of play from *Absurd Person Singular*.

Very often a play has failed because the audience was

led to expect one sort of play and then given another – such as a comedy that turned into romantic fantasy or (as can more easily happen) toppled into farce. Obviously it is not a good idea to have your hero commit suicide at the end of a comedy or indulge in throwing custard pies in the middle of a drama, but the mistakes need not be as obvious as that to alienate the audience. They may merely leave the theatre with a vague impression that all is not quite as it should be – in other words less than satisfied; and a dissatisfied audience is to be avoided. True, there is a very effective scene with comic gravediggers towards the end of *Hamlet*, but this merely lightens the mood before the wholesale slaughter that is to follow (this is an object lesson in audience manipulation) and the writing from the very first lines of the play displays a consistent sardonic sense of humour.

So is what follows to be a thriller, a fantasy, theatre of the absurd, nostalgic romance, or what? The audience must be advised what to expect if it is trust the writer later.

What is the *style* to be? That is the style of the play, not the author's writing style, which should be as individual as a tone of voice (Shakespeare is recognizably Shakespeare whether writing *Twelfth Night* or *King Lear*; Alans Bennett and Ayckbourn have written both dark and light plays, but their tone of voice is unmistakable.) The question at its simplest is: naturalistic or otherwise?

Naturalism keeps up the pretence of a fourth wall – the invisible one between actors and audience. A bargain is struck – we all know that we are in a theatre, but we will pretend that we are not. We in the audience will assume that the action on stage is for real and that we are eavesdropping on characters speaking the language of the living-room, office, pub and bus stop. They behave as real people in those surroundings would. (If they should express themselves more wittily or lucidly than we might that is part of the magic of theatre.) But they do not without very good reason break into blank verse, make wildly extravagant gestures, burst into song or talk to the audience – any more than at home we normally talk to ourselves or start addressing the fireplace.

Naturalism is still the style most used in the theatre, and

even more so in films and television. It may seem simpler to write. After all you only have to make the characters talk and behave the way everyone around you is talking and behaving. Even improbable events can be made to seem probable when surrounded by naturalistic detail: if everything else on stage is so real, then the story can be swallowed too. This is a great help when writing a thriller for instance.

It has the *dis*advantage of having difficulty in getting beyond that convincing surface, in making really big gestures without seeming silly – if they become too extravagant the audience may laugh at what should be a serious moment. Perhaps the biggest disadvantage comes from the difficulty in getting characters to say what they are really thinking. This has to be conveyed *between* the lines through hints, hesitations and pauses. (Read the plays of Rattigan and Coward to find out how experts conveyed what could not be said.)

A non-naturalistic play calls for a different understanding. Here there is an agreement that the audience is watching actors on stage performing a play. A non-naturalistic play allows more opportunity for the use of such theatrical devices as talking directly to the audience, moving freely through time and space, and changing characters with the change of a hat. It involves greater use of an element of 'let's pretend'. The Chorus in *Henry V* says, 'Think when we talk of horses that you see them,' and we do. In Thornton Wilder's *The Happy Journey* an actor puts four chairs together, tells the audience that this is a car, and the audience accepts that it is being driven from Trenton to Camden. In his *Long Christmas Dinner* the action covers a lifetime while the characters sit at a table laid for dinner. In Jarry's *Ubu Roi* the entire Polish army is represented by one actor. In Planchon's adaptation of *The Three Musketeers* D'Artagnan says to the audience, 'It takes three days to get to Paris.... Three days later ...' and three days have gone by in mid-speech.

Pantomime is a prime example of non-naturalistic theatre. Men play women and girls play boys. Animals talk. Performers talk to the audience and the audience answers back. Music is an important element.

Although naturalism is an ideal medium for psychological studies, characters in non-naturalistic theatre are not less three-dimensional, nor their problems less real. Mother Courage is larger than life, dealing with matters of life and death as she trades with soldiers during the Thirty Years War. That play could hardly have been conceived naturalistically – any more than Rattigan's *The Browning Version*, with its introspective schoolmaster protagonist, would have been effective except behind the imaginary fourth wall.

Broadly speaking, naturalistic theatre is best when dealing with the details of everyday life, non-naturalistic theatre with a broader sweep of ideas. Decide which best suits your story – then stick to it. Don't create confusion by changing conventions in mid-play. Gain the confidence of your audience by making clear from the start what you intend, then do just that. From the first scene on.

Try to set the tone of the play from the very opening. *Macbeth* starts with witches on a blasted heath, and *Hamlet* on battlements at night with sentries waiting apprehensively for the appearance of a ghost. Both are gory dramas with heavy overtones of the supernatural, and after those openings we are conditioned to accept what follows. *Twelfth Night* on the other hand opens to music and the line 'If music be the food of love, play on'. It sets the mood for a romantic comedy. In almost every major play the first lines signpost what is to come.

Some more modern examples.... Pinter's *The Caretaker* opens without dialogue. Mick is sitting alone; a distant door bangs; Mick gets up and walks out; Aston and Davies enter talking, but Mick is never mentioned. An odd climate of unanswered questions and unspoken meanings is set up in that first minute. Christopher Fry's *The Lady's Not for Burning* opens with Thomas Mendip addressing a copying-clerk through the open window.

THOMAS: Soul!

RICHARD: – and   the   plasterer,   that's   fifteen
                  groats –

THOMAS: Hey, soul!

RICHARD: – for stopping the draught in the privy –

THOMAS: Body!
                        You calculating piece of clay.

What follows can hardly help being a comedy, and our ears are already being tuned to expect anything but everyday speech. The 'groats' even advises us that it will not be taking place in the present day. Alan Bennett's *A Question of Attribution* is about the fourth man in a spy scandal, but Bennett is less concerned with Le Carré or Deighton intrigue as with character. So it opens, not with a scene between Blunt and the Man from M.I.5 (which would have indicated a story of espionage) but between Blunt and a picture restorer discussing an old-master painting of two men (in which hidden portraits of a third and fourth man are later discovered). This way he avoids pointing audiences in the wrong direction – or even allowing them to jump to wrong conclusions about the sort of play that is to follow.

A thriller need not necessarily start with screams and gunshots, or a farce by throwing a bucket of whitewash; but do make the best of those first minutes for starting the play on the right foot.

At the other end of the play the final scene should sum up all that has gone before – not only the story but also the feeling and intention of the play. So *Macbeth* ends not merely with the tyrant dead, but with Malcolm triumphantly announcing his forthcoming coronation. *Twelfth Night* ends with a rather wistful song from the clown, Feste: there have been knockabout scenes of comedy but the play was a *romantic* comedy.

Between the curtain first rising and finally falling, the attention of the audience must be held. There are many ways of doing this but the most important are the uses of clarity and suspense.

Of these clarity comes first, because real suspense cannot be achieved without it. If you were to encounter a collision between two cars, your attitude would immediately become more concerned if you realized that you knew one of the drivers. If you also found out that the car had for instance been rushing a patient urgently to hospital, you would become even more concerned. In other words the more you knew about the situation, the more you would be drawn into the action. A frequent failing in early plays is that too little information is given and too late.

An illustration (from a play that has yet to be written)....
A man and a girl sit not too close to each other in a bar. They say very little except to exchange routine banalities about the weather. If that is all we in the audience know about them, boredom will soon set in. On the other hand if we have already been told that the girl is expecting to meet a blind date and is not quite sure whether the man is the one, interest is aroused. If we have also been told that (blind date or not) the man is a homicidal psychopath, suspense will be considerably increased. On the surface the situation is a bore but, if we have been put completely in the picture, without adding or changing a word or gesture, it becomes gripping.

This is not to say that at the beginning of a whodunit the detective should announce that the butler did it. A writer is entitled to decide when to reveal surprises or even to keep some secrets (Did Eliza marry Higgins? Who is Godot?) but an audience should be given at least the minimum information needed to understand what is happening on stage *at any given moment*. (At the beginning of *Arsenic and Old Lace* it was only necessary for the writer to reveal that Martha and Abby Brewster were sweet old ladies: the fact that they were poisoners could wait.)

This supply of information should start from the moment the play begins. Let the audience know as soon as possible where, when, who and what.

Where is the action taking place? A lot can be conveyed immediately by the setting, including lighting and sound effects. The crazy old house in Brooklyn in which the Brewster sisters live is revealed as soon as the curtain rises – complete with stairs up which Teddy Brewster will charge and doors down to the cellar where the bodies are buried. The state of the apartment in which Oscar lives in *The Odd Couple* not only tells us where he lives, but how. In my own *The Laboratory* a Renaissance alchemist's cellar is lit by candles and a glow from the furnace. At the start of Molnar's *Lilliom* music can be heard from a distant amusement park. Characters may augment this with action or dialogue. In *Barefoot in the Park* they enter exhausted, having climbed flights of stairs to the top apartment. Hannah on the phone at the opening of *California Suite* says, 'Come on up ... room 203.'

Time should be allowed for this information to be absorbed before anything of importance in the story is said or done. The time needed will depend on how much there is to absorb. If the stage picture is elaborate more time will be needed than for a simple setting. The process can be helped if the writer is able to draw attention to items most likely to catch the attention of the audience. Once they have been noted they cease to be objects of curiosity. To use the previously mentioned *The Laboratory* as an example – the stage is cluttered with alchemical apparatus and dominated by a furnace on which pots bubble and simmer. An apothecary sits writing by the light of a candle with a skull on his desk. He reads what he has just written aloud to the skull (but does not expect an answer) then, having referred to the potions near the fire, potters over to it to inspect them. After this the audience has been conditioned to let the background be just that and to concentrate on the play. With a bare stage Shakespeare was able to plunge straight into the action – though he was always careful to establish what was happening and where.

Who are the characters? What is their basic relationship to each other? This is comparatively easy to establish because we tend to include names and/or terms of endearment naturally in our conversation. One person addressing another as Sir, Dear, Sweet, or Hey-You immediately establishes a relationship. Attitudes vary according to the status of the person dealt with – higher, lower or equal (a chapter of Keith Johnstone's book *Impro* is devoted to just that trait – as well as containing some excellent advice on playwriting). If they are relevant, try to include names early in a scene. Avoid excessive name-dropping, though: it is not necessary to start or finish each speech with a name in order to establish who is speaking to whom.

Unless otherwise informed, audiences have a way of

making certain basic assumptions about characters – boy and girl together must be in love, man and woman quarrelling must be married. (Henri Becque made use of this assumption for a celebrated dramatic twist in *La Parisienne*, which opens with a domestic row – at the end of which an off-stage door bangs and the woman exclaims, 'My husband!') In *The Devil's Disciple* when Dick Dudgeon allowed himself to be arrested instead of Anderson, audiences assumed it was because he and Mrs Anderson were lovers. This irritated Shaw, but the fault was his: he should have done more earlier to counter that assumption. If the relationships between your characters are anything but obvious, clarify the true state of affairs as soon as possible.

When the action happens may not be so vital; though unless advised otherwise, an audience will assume that it is taking place in the present day. Time and date can usually be suggested more or less subtly by setting, lighting and by what is happening – tea in the afternoon, breakfast in the morning, etc. J.M. Barrie's *The Will* takes place in a solicitor's office, in which the furniture remains the same throughout the play; but it opens with a picture of Queen Victoria prominent on the wall. For the next two scenes this is changed successively to King Edward VII and King George V, immediately indicating the passage of years. In the first act of *A Doll's House* Nora arrives home with a Christmas tree and at the opening of the second act the tree stands stripped and bedraggled with its candles burned out: Christmas is over.

A successful play of the 1930s was *Ten Minute Alibi*, the plot of which hinged on the passing of time. So an essential part of the setting was a large modern clock with a square face and large hands and numerals. Unfortunately this meant that, all the time the play was in progress, someone had to be employed moving those hands minute by minute. If your story demands a clock, try to arrange matters so that it faces away from the audience – otherwise they may either be wondering why the hands are not moving or contrariwise wondering how it is done. Either way concentration will suffer.

What happened before the play started? As it were, 'the

story so far'. The word frequently used for this is exposition: which is merely the same as putting the audience in the picture.

As a play must necessarily be happening in the present, one disadvantage in catching up with the past is that everything else may grind to a halt while this is being done. As far as possible this should be given in dramatic terms. The dullest way is merely to allow the audience to eavesdrop on two people. Any number of bad old plays start with a totally undramatic conversation between two servants; though this boring opening is not unknown in some bad new plays either (even when the playwright tries to disguise the lack of drama with a series of jokes). *Never* have two people telling each other what both know perfectly well already. Even Shakespeare nods in the first scene of *The Winter's Tale* where two courtiers tell each other what they have been observing together for the past few months. One has the feeling that, near the end of his working life, the old master was becoming impatient with routine problems of exposition and was saying in effect 'to hell with them, let's get on with the play'. In his last play, *The Tempest*, there is also a stodgy and improbable scene between Prospero and Miranda in which a father explains to his daughter how they came to be marooned on the island – after twelve years of living there together!

Information should always flow from the character who knows to the one who does not. To be really dramatic the one who does not know should be trying to get information from one who does not want to give it. Which is the formula for many detective stories, besides containing the basic ingredients for a dramatic situation: someone wants something and is prevented from getting it.

There may be a doubtful compromise when characters get together to reminisce – in which case they will still be talking of things known to both, but will at least have a reason. This can be a bland and potentially boring way of giving details about the past, unless the situation itself contains elements of drama – as when the family in J.B. Priestley's *The Linden Tree* recall holidays when they were all much younger: a happy scene, the mood of which is soon about to be shattered. Or characters could have difficulty in remembering and disagree over what is remembered (as in the *Gigi* duet between Hermione Gingold and Maurice Chevalier.)

The past does not necessarily all have to be disclosed in one indigestible chunk. The information can be spread over several scenes. If the interest of the audience can be aroused so that they actually want to know, so much the better. An otherwise rather dull patch of exposition can be made acceptable if the audience can actually be made to ask for it.

In special circumstances, particularly where there is so much to be explained that the play would be in danger of coming to a full stop, a flashback may be used. This is a scene from the past, played as though it were in the present. My *Dead and Alive* is told in a series of flashbacks as a detective questions a suspect about four inexplicable deaths. In the thirties whodunit *I Killed the Count*, the story of each suspect is told in flashback; and the second act of *Black Limelight* is wholly taken up with showing how a murder was committed. (Odd that the thriller should seem to make more use of the technique than other sorts of play.) Arthur Miller's *Death of a Salesman* is a constant blending of past and present. However a flashback can be technically tricky to stage, and is liable to interrupt the forward thrust of a story, so it should be used only when absolutely necessary and then with great care.

For the sake of clarity the audience will need to be put in possession of essential information, not only as part of being brought up to date, at the beginning or after a scene break, but also continually throughout the play.

It is more effective and less time-consuming to prepare in advance than to explain afterwards. If a vital bridge is to be swept away in a storm, let it be known that the bridge is not exactly sound and that a storm could be brewing. If your heroine is to defend herself with a paper-knife snatched from her desk, the audience should have known the knife was there. If not, disbelief can set in. Worse, such a convenient appearance of the weapon can produce a feeling of being cheated. When this information is given before it is actually used, the process is known as planting.

A plant is something that can be looked back on for corroboration. What Pooh-Bah described as, 'detail, intended to give artistic verisimilitude to an otherwise bald and unconvincing narrative'. Or it can be a way of preparing an audience to accept later events and react to them in the way the writer wants.

Planting can be done in words – one character telling another for example, 'I always wear that coat when I go shopping'. So we are not surprised when the coat in question turns up at the scene of the crime.

Or in action – for example, a character takes a piece of paper from his pocket and hides it up the chimney. As actions speak louder than words, where possible show. There will be more impact if a situation is demonstrated rather than talked about. If two characters are seen embracing, then the assumption is that they are not strangers; if one knocks the other down, a fair deduction can be made that they are not on the best of terms.

Or a plant may be merely something seen or heard – a picture prominently placed like the portrait in *The Will* or James Bridie's *Doctor Angelus*, or the sound of church bells outside as at the opening of *Look Back in Anger*.

A plant at times needs to be unobtrusive. If certain information is given too obviously, an audience may actually be waiting for it to be used. In the case of the previously mentioned paper-knife, if a character were to remark, 'What a sharp knife that is. You could do a lot of damage with a blade like that', so much attention would be drawn to it that suspense would be lost when the heroine was in danger. (Though the remark would be legitimate if, instead of the knife merely being handy opportunely, there was deliberate intention to raise suspense by having the audience wonder *when* it was going to be used.)

If the way in which information is to be used is not to be obvious, it can be introduced in the way a conjurer works – in a different context. The audience sees, but with luck does not immediately appreciate the significance of what it has seen. Again using the previous example, the knife might have been observed during the forcing of a lock or cleaning a pipe: establishing it, but not as an offensive weapon. In *Dial 'M' for Murder* the scissors with which the villain is stabbed are seen being used earlier when the heroine is clipping out newspaper cuttings for her husband's scrap-book.

Another example of ingenious planting is Eliza's 'bloody' in *Pygmalion*. In an earlier scene Mrs Pearce complains about Eliza using the word in connection with the bath water, and asks Higgins to stop using it himself. So when it comes out in the middle of a polite tea party, it is not only unexpected in that context, but it has been prepared for. The audience makes the connection and the laugh is much bigger than a casual swear-word would have been. (The equivalent scene in *My Fair Lady* falls rather flat because what Eliza says at Ascot has not been prepared for.)

Remember that a plant should occur before an event. If a writer finds it necessary to give reasons after something has happened, then the chances are that it has been insufficiently planted earlier. Instead of dramatic tension being lost by backward-looking explanations an audience should be saying, 'Ah, yes. Of course' as the event happens. Or, if the playwright has been really ingenious, 'We didn't expect that – but we ought to have done.'

Planting can be used for certain special purposes.

Characterization can be deepened and rounded by appropriate planting. The better an audience feels it knows a character, the more it will become involved with that character. We form our opinion of people from what we see them say and do, and from what others say about them.

It is not sufficient merely to describe a person in a stage direction as mean, brave, flighty, or generous. The character must be seen to demonstrate those traits in as many ways as possible, from small gestures to major decisions. Richard III tells us that his brother is top of his hit list of victims and immediately afterwards, meeting that brother on his way to prison, is full of sympathy and brotherly love. A little later he meets the widow of a man he has killed and, by the side of the victim's coffin, persuades her to marry him. After this we do not need to be told that Richard is devious, ruthless and has an outstanding gift for persuasion. We have seen it for ourselves. Moreover from his asides we in the audience can appreciate his quirky sense of humour – 'Was ever woman in this humour wooed?/Was ever woman in this humour won?'

Higgins in *Pygmalion* is a bad-mannered bully. To her face he calls Eliza, among other insults, a 'draggle-tailed guttersnipe'; he peremptorily orders Mrs Pearce to bath Eliza and burn her clothes; he insults his mother's guests.

Having another character give an independent opinion can also plant a trait. Queen Margaret calls Richard 'a bottled spider'. Eliza says to Higgins, 'Oh, you've no feeling heart in you: you don't care for nothing but yourself.' At the same time, of course, the persons speaking are helping to characterize themselves.

Careful planting can make characters attractive who might otherwise be anything but. Higgins has boundless enthusiasm for his chosen subject of phonetics, and he is generous – he empties his pockets into Eliza's basket. Note how the lethal Brewster sisters in *Arsenic and Old Lace* are made acceptable. They are elderly and vulnerable particularly when contrasted with their really nasty brother, psychopathic killer Jonathan. They have strict religious principles (holding funeral services over their victims). They collect toys for the children's Christmas Fund and distribute soup to the sick and needy. Moreover they consider the poisoning of lonely old gentlemen to be one of their philanthropic activities. Motivation is important to character.

Motivation, the reason why people behave the way they do, should also be well planted. This is usually tied in with the story-line anyway. A character has to do a certain thing or the play would come to a halt; but the audience should be able to see (or at least deduce) *why* that thing is done. For instance your story may require a bank clerk to steal a fortune; in which case you should have planted that he was the sort of person who might steal it, that he had a pressing reason to steal it, and that he had access to it. One really good motive (demonstrated if necessary in several ways) is better than a number of less compulsive motives. Iago in *Othello* rather suffers from this – does he destroy Othello from envy, on racist grounds, for revenge on account of being passed over for promotion or merely because he delights in making mischief? All these motives are planted, but are together less convincing than just one given more prominence would have been.

The atmosphere of a scene can be enhanced by planting background details. These need not necessarily have a direct effect on the action but may add to its impact. What season is it? – high summer or bleak mid-winter? *The Lady's Not for Burning* takes place on a day in spring; the last act of *Cyrano de Bergerac* on a day in October. What time of day is it? Would breakfast or midnight be the best time for a revelation of infidelity? What is the weather like? Imagine the difference bright sunlight or wind and rain would make. The storm on the heath does not change the course of events in *Lear*, but it increases the effect of the King losing his mind. Towards the end of *The Merchant of Venice* Lorenzo and Jessica could have arrived at Belmont in the midday sun, instead of which the romance of the scene is increased by moonlight and distant music.

Planting is a process that takes place automatically when an experienced playwright is working, but almost any play can be improved by the careful addition of plants after the first draft, (plays are not written but rewritten) because although the writer may have a clear personal picture of what is happening, that picture may not always be conveyed so clearly to the audience. With practice it is possible to learn where planting is most effective.

One word of warning. While at all times making sure that the audience has been told all that it needs to know, beware of trying to feed too much too soon. Major points take time to be digested. One in three to five minutes is probably as much as an audience can be expected to absorb. Going back to *The Mikado*, in the first scene we are told that Nanki-Poo is looking for Yum-Yum, in the following scene we are told that she is to be married to Ko-Ko, two scenes later Nanki-Poo reveals himself to be the son of the Mikado. Each important fact is given time to sink in before Gilbert goes on to the next.

6 Suspense

Suspense is what keeps audiences involved until the writer is ready to let them go. (In particular bringing them back to their seats after an interval.) At the most basic level this means getting them to ask, 'What is going to happen?' or in the case of a well-known story, 'We know what, but *how* is it going to happen?'

A question mark should hang over the futures of the characters involved if we are to care what happens to them (and if we are not made to care then everybody in the theatre is wasting time). A play progresses in a series of questions raised and answered. These become bigger and more vital as the play goes on until the biggest question of all is finally answered.

Will Hamlet avenge his father's murder? Yes.

Will Davies be installed as caretaker? No.

Will Charles Condomine get rid of the ghosts of his wives? Yes.

Will Tony Wendyce succeed in getting his wife hanged for murder? No.

Will Ralph Clark manage to stage 'The Recruiting Officer'? Yes.

And once the big question has been answered, the main action is over.

In order to be able to ask those questions the issues, with possible alternatives (what will be the consequence if Charles does not exorcize Elvira, what will happen if Tony Wendyce's plan should succeed), should be clearly understood (clarity again); and so that they can be clearly *understood* they must be clearly *presented* in dramatic terms as a series of crises and climaxes.

For our purposes let us define a crisis as a point in the

action at which an issue is in doubt and a climax as the point at which a crisis is resolved (so the issue is no longer in doubt).

First the situation has to be shown before the problem arises – the *status quo*. For instance at the opening of *Hamlet* we see the Court of Denmark behaving as normally as may be expected after a change of leader. Even Hamlet reluctantly accepts the situation. Then he learns that his uncle murdered his father. Hamlet's life is disrupted: what is he to do? By the time the final question has been resolved, all the leading characters are dead, Fortinbras has taken over the country and a new regime begins....

At the beginning of *Arsenic and Old Lace* we see Mortimer Brewster about to be married and his aunts going about their normal philanthropic business. (*Status quo*.) Then he learns that the cellar is full of bodies, poisoned by the aunts who brought him up and for whom he cares. What is he to do? By the end of the play the aunts have agreed to go into a home and Mortimer realizes that he is not related to psychopaths after all. He is free to marry and his aunts are taken care of. A new *status quo*.

This sequence is repeated in miniature in single scenes as in the complete outline of a play. A situation is first established as normal; something happens to upset it; in particular somebody wants something and something is in the way of their getting what they want (crisis) and, after dealing with complications, they either get what they want or clearly do not (climax), and at the end a new situation is established. As far as that particular scene is concerned the issue has been settled (though the struggle may be taken up again later in the course of the action).

As a really crude example imagine a shop or bank with the person behind the counter working normally. A robber enters and points a gun with an order to hand over money. Crisis. The victim either hands over the money or doesn't and is shot; or sounds an alarm and the gunman runs off empty-handed. The victim may even turn the tables and shoot the robber. At all events by the end of the scene the situation is resolved. Climax. And we have a new situation to which everyone previously involved adjusts.

At the risk of confusing a simple definition, a climax itself can become a new crisis. The robber gets the money (climax to this scene) but now there arises the question of whether he will get away with it (further crisis arising from that climax). Alternatively the victim resolves the situation by shooting the robber. (Climax.) But will the robber live? (Crisis.)

Richard accepts the crown but can he keep it?

Romeo marries Juliet, but is exiled from Verona.

Eliza is passed off as an aristocrat, but what is to become of her now?

Within each unit (of *status quo*, crisis, and re-established *status quo*) there may be a number of complications to delay the final resolution. Each complication increases the tension by postponing the climax. In the instance above, if the robber were in a bank the gun might get stuck in his pocket; he might have difficulty in finding the note demanding the money; he may have just come in from a storm to discover the rain has washed the ink from the paper on which the demand was written; the cashier may not be able to read it; when he comes to say what he wants, the robber may have caught cold and lost his voice; he may have forgotten to load the gun; other customers may try to push him out of the queue; the cashier may refuse to pay and threaten to sound the alarm; and so on....

From this example it will be seen that complications can arise from many directions:

the characters directly involved. An incompetent gunman, an obstinate cashier

the situation itself – the cashier refuses to pay

the background – banks have alarms

the weather – rain ruins the note

peripheral characters otherwise unconnected with the story – other customers get in the way

even accident – the robber could shoot himself in the foot.

There is an infinity of choices, don't be afraid to explore them.

The reason why the first attempts of many playwrights seem so thin is because they fail to recognize the dramatic possibilities in a situation. If a play seems too short they are tempted to pad with extra dialogue leading nowhere rather than investigate possible complications related to the situation. After a few minutes' consideration the possible complications to such a simple action as making a pot of tea could fill a page.

The number and intensity of crises will depend on the sort of play. There are likely to be more in a farce or action thriller than in a gentle comedy or psychological drama.

Nor need they involve physical action. In a courtroom drama for instance the issues are clearly laid out from the start – is the accused guilty or not guilty? – and dealt with entirely through argument, interrogation or pleading. (Perhaps this clear definition of what is at stake accounts for the popularity of this sort of play.) In romantic comedy the progress may be almost entirely verbal.

Beware of progressing in a series of small crises of almost equal importance and which when dealt with add nothing to the larger question. (All the smaller units are like building blocks contributing to a main structure. Never lose sight of the complete outline with its major issues to be resolved.) Many adventure films have this structure – the hero swims a river, then tracks through a forest, then fights off an unfriendly tribe, then crosses a desert, and so on and on. Film, though, is a different medium, with other devices for holding the attention of an audience.

Crises should increase in importance as the play progresses. If the most important issue is decided too early in a full-length play, the audience will have less incentive to return to their seats after the interval. If only for this reason it is advisable to have a major crisis just before the interval. And a period of recovery after the break while threads are picked up again and the audience reminded of the issues.

Playwrights frequently fail to achieve maximum tension with a dramatic situation because these elements of crisis, complication and climax are not fully developed. A scene is either finished too quickly or even broken off before the climax has been reached. As though in a bank robbery the cashier were to hand over the money without question or the robber were to change his mind and make a small deposit instead.

While this is happening it is important that the audience should always be kept aware of the issues involved. In effect the playwright should be telling them what to look for. Pointing them in the right direction.

Pointing, as with planting, is a continuous process throughout the play and there are many ways of doing it.

Direct statement: Madam in *Little Brother, Little Sister* says, 'We must go outside'. Richard III tells the audience that he is going to do away with anyone who stands between him and the crown. Irina in *The Three Sisters* says, 'To go to Moscow!' In fact any character who says 'I want'.

Threats, promises, boasts or pleas: Higgins boasts that he can pass off a flower-girl as a duchess. Cinderella pleads with her stepsisters to be allowed to go to the ball. Any Western villain who threatens, 'Get out of town, or else'. The Soothsayer warns Julius Caesar, 'Beware the Ides of March'. Perhaps the most famous of all is the warning to Cinderella to be home by midnight.

The circumstances of the story can themselves act as a pointer. In the 'and then there were none' formula, when characters are disposed of one by one, the audience knows that the mayhem will go on until only the hero/heroine and the villain are left, and will be waiting for the next victim to drop dead. Even one quite ignorant of history, after the meetings of conspirators, will be waiting for an assassination attempt on Caesar.

The relationship between characters can point to future developments. The most common is boy meets girl. When Romeo meets Juliet there is no need to be told to watch out for a romantic entanglement. (And the relationship between Tybalt and Romeo points to an inevitable clash between that pair.) Shaw denied any romantic involvement between Eliza and Higgins, but everything in the story points towards it so that, in spite of the author's protestations, the audience knows that they must be united at the end.

Delays or interruptions can add emphasis to what is pointed. The Porter's delay in opening the door in *Macbeth* directs attention to the murder because the discovery is being held up. The importance of even a simple action, such as making a telephone call, will be increased if it is repeatedly interrupted.

Time limits add to suspense. It is a staple of melodrama – from the heroine who must be rescued from the railway track before the 10.15 passes, to the bomb that is timed to explode at noon.

Stage business or technical effects can act as pointers. Moving an article or piece of furniture draws attention to it. In *Blithe Spirit* Charles starts to object to the use of the record of 'Always'. A difference in lighting does the same. If for instance a picture were prominently displayed, or lit more intensely than any other part of the stage, attention would be drawn to it. If afterwards it were to play no significant part in the action, the audience would be justified in feeling let down.

So be on the look-out for false pointers. Beware of creating unfulfilled expectations. (As Shaw failed to do with Higgins and Eliza: there was a similar lapse, too, in *The Devil's Disciple* where inadequate motivation is given for Dick allowing himself to be arrested.) You may even have to make a point of emphasizing when something is *not* intended.

If pointers have been correctly placed, certain scenes will be expected by the audience. One of these will almost inevitably be the climax of the play. As Stanley says in *A Streetcar Named Desire*, 'We've had this date with each other from the beginning.' In some old text books these scenes are referred to as Obligatory Scenes. In other words the scenes you are obliged to write if you do not want the audience to feel cheated. Such a scene can only be avoided if there is a clear understanding that it will take place, even if off-stage. Such as the scene at the very end of *Dial 'M' For Murder*, when the curtain falls on Wendyce turning a key in the door that will open to reveal the police waiting for him to make just that one false move. In this case the audience knows exactly what is going to happen after the curtain falls, so the inevitable arrest can be suggested rather than stated. But do not use this device as a way of dodging away from a confrontation that has been promised.

Don't forget that the climax of a play may not coincide with the last scene. In *The Barretts of Wimpole Street* the last section is taken up by the effect on the Barrett household of Elizabeth's elopement. Time may be needed to demonstrate the new *status quo* that has been established after the climax. It may not be sufficient merely to say, 'They lived happily ever after': the writer may need to *show* them living happily ever after (or not as the case may be).

Just as the first scene should put the audience in the right mood for what is to come, the last scene should sum up all that has gone before: what the playwright feels about it and, more importantly what the audience is expected to feel about it.

This could be called The Theme, but the word 'theme' suggests a didactic sort of statement such as 'Crime does not pay' or 'A rolling stone gathers no moss' – in other words a 'message'. Messages are risky if only because the play may become distorted to carry the message instead of being true to the characters and story-line. Plays with a purpose have been successful – Galsworthy's *Strife* and *Justice*, Odets' *Waiting For Lefty*, Miller's *The Crucible*, Irwin Shaw's *Bury the Dead* to name a handful, but in these plays there is no feeling of characters and incidents being forced to fit an idea the writer wanted to put over. When James Bridie was asked if a play could have a message, he replied, 'Certainly – as long as you don't let the characters know what it is.' At the dress rehearsal of an amateur production one of my plays, *Incident*, (and after working on it for several weeks) the director rushed up to me saying, 'I've only just realized – this play is about racial discrimination'. I was flattered to think that I had made my point – at the right time.

The idea that a play should have a theme started with the Greek critic Aristotle when he included it as one of the six elements necessary to a play. (The others were plot, characters, language, visual impact, and music: how much has changed in the theatre since 330 BC? – worth thinking about.) There has to be something in that slot pointed out by Aristotle, but it might better be described as Author's Attitude. Not so much 'This is what you ought to believe' as 'This is my point of view. This is why I wrote the play.' By the end of the play an audience should be seeing the world through the playwright's eyes. (One reason why a writer should be scrupulously honest, especially when writing fiction: it can be very revealing – prevarication and insincerity tend to show through.)

Sometimes words are inadequate for summing up a play. We are left with something more like an emotion – such as that conjured up by the ending of *The Cherry Orchard*, with the house empty and the sound outside of axes hacking away at the trees: the feeling that a whole way of life is coming to an end. Or the dug-out at the end of *Journey's End*, with the body of Raleigh lying alone and the sound of the guns outside.

The ending of a play is what audiences take away with them. In spite of the misery and squalor that precedes it, the finale of *Our Country's Good* is a triumphant production of *The Recruiting Officer*, a tribute to the resilience of the human spirit. When Anouilh and Shaw came to write the story of Joan of Arc in *The Lark* and *Saint Joan*, they realized that their plays could not end with her death. Anouilh ended with a flashback to the Dauphin's coronation, the peak of Joan's career, and Shaw had an epilogue flashing forward to her canonization. The ending of *The Trojan War Will Not Take Place* is doubly ironic because everyone knows from the start that the Trojan War has to take place; but Giraudoux makes it take place, not on account of negotiations for Helen's return breaking down, but because of a ridiculous accident (the possibility of which had been carefully planted) emphasizing the stupidity of war as a means of settling differences. On a lighter note, at the end of *Private Lives*, Elyot and Amanda slip away while their spouses quarrel. They belong together. All these endings are right for their plays. With the wrong ending the audience may take away something the writer had not intended.

Inexperienced playwrights seem to favour inconclusive

endings; in effect saying, 'These are the facts, let the
audience decide'. But a play is not a debate. It may
possibly end with a question mark (*Saint Joan* ends with,
'How long, O Lord? How long?') especially if the writer
really wants the audience to believe that a problem to be
insoluble. However they are much more likely to leave
totally confused, wondering why the play stopped there, a
state of mind boding ill for its success. Rather than being
an example of impartiality, the inconclusive ending is
much more likely to come over as an example of sloppy
thinking.

The ending of a play should in retrospect seem to be not
only right, but inevitable. This is one of the strengths of
Greek tragedy. (Anouilh remarks in his adaptation of the
Greek *Antigone*, 'Tragedy ... is restful'.) Not only classic
tragedy, though. Think about some modern plays – *The
Caretaker, Death of a Salesman, The Crucible....*

It is not necessary to construct a play backwards – to
decide on the ending and then work out the story-line in
reverse; but it is a good idea to look back once you have
reached that point, see whether you have said what you
set out to say and make sure that the audience has been
prepared for it.

7 Scene by Scene

At last! This is what a play should look like on the page. When submitting a play to managers, theatres, publishers, or agents in the UK a script should be laid out like this:

ACT ONE

Scene Two

(Mary's living-room. It is furnished with comfortable, if rather worn, easy chairs and there is a painted fire-screen on the hearth.

Early evening sunshine streams through open french windows.

MARY is arranging flowers in a large vase and singing happily to herself.

Outside a car horn sounds viciously. MARY ignores it.

The door is suddenly flung open. RON stamps in, throws a brief case into one chair and slumps into another.)

MARY: *(without turning)* Is that you, dear?

RON: Who were you expecting?

MARY: I was rather hoping for a charming stranger who would sweep me into his arms and crush me to him with passionate kisses. But I suppose I'll have to make do with you.

(*She crosses to him and tickles his ear with a flower.*)

RON: (*pushing her away*) Never – do that – with a dahlia. They're infested with earwigs.

MARY: Sorry.

RON: (*rubbing his ear*) Why a stranger?

MARY: (*returning to her vase*) Because it would have been too much to hope for from any of the men in my life.

RON: Men?

MARY: It wouldn't be quite the same with a woman.

RON: Is there more than one man in your life?

MARY: Oh, lots. By the way your dinner's in the oven. I think it passed the point of no return half an hour ago.

(*She goes out with the flower arrangement.*)

RON: My –? (*He jumps up.*) What did you mean by …?

(*He dashes after her.*)

Notice how:

The characters' names are written down the left side of the page.

The dialogue is clearly indented. Spacing is double between the speeches, with single spacing between the lines in any one speech.

Stage directions are indented even further and italicized or underlined. The script is set out in this way for easy reading so that at a glance one can see who is speaking, and that what they are doing is not confused with what they say.

Each new scene should each be started on a new page.

When a script is set out in this way each department

involved in putting on a play will be able to see at a glance what they are required to do. The set designer should get an idea of the stage picture; the lighting and sound experts will be told where their cues will come; the property manager can start to make a shopping list of the more esoteric items. And of course the actors will know what to say and do.

Note that the present tense is always used in stage directions. This is because a theatrical performance can only take place in the present. (A sound recording, film or video may preserve something that happened in the past, but even while being recorded for posterity the action was taking place in the present.)

Also note that the dialogue in a play is not enclosed in inverted commas as it usually is in a story, because a play is *expected* to be in dialogue. This is only a tiny point, but I am sometimes asked to judge playwriting competitions and by now I have stopped being surprised by the number of entries in which those inverted commas appear. Though of course they should still be used for their other function of quote-unquote, and to indicate to a performer that a word should be given a special inflexion, usually expressing doubt, for example:

JUDGE: Where did you 'find' this handbag?

When writing down stage directions try to say precisely what you want to be seen on stage, but say no more than is necessary. Allow for flexibility and let other departments get on with their jobs: after all that is what they are paid to do.

Remember that actors are trained to say lines and to interpret character. There is usually no need to give them notes on how to deliver a line, for example:

CHARLES: (*sadly*) My grandmother died today.

Such a note is necessary only if there is something special about the delivery, such as, *bewildered*, or if it is contrary to a normal interpretation of the line such as, *laughing uproariously*.

The same applies to stage 'business' (what the actors

do). There is little point in writing, *Meditatively chewing the end of a pencil*, if the director has decided not to use a pencil. The actor may even think of a better way to convey the mood than by pencil chewing (beating an egg, perhaps, or tearing a telephone directory in half) but then be inhibited from suggesting it because you have asked for that pencil.

Coaxing performances from the cast is one of the jobs of the play's director. Another is responsibility for the stage picture – the way performers are grouped and move. So such embellishments as, *Strides manfully to the fireplace and drapes himself in an imposing attitude against the mantelpiece* are not only irrelevant, but may also cause the director to skip other directions – *Surreptitiously searching the drawer for a gun* – that may be more important.

Some directors make a point of never reading stage directions. One such, when asked what he would do if a character were to die on stage without any reference to the fact in the dialogue, remarked, 'Probably wonder why they'd stopped speaking'.

At the first rehearsal of one of my plays the director was obviously having difficulty with the grouping. At the coffee break he took me aside and suggested that some rewriting was in order because, no matter how he moved the actors, one character was always where he shouldn't be. When I pointed out that half the action took place in a living-room and the other half in the kitchen and that there was a wall between the two, light dawned. He had not even read the description of the setting. It *was* theatre-in-the-round though, with minimal furnishings – and later he went on to include a sink with taps that really produced water and a telephone from which the dialogue at the other end of the line could also be heard, which is more than I as the author would have dared to suggest.

During rehearsals of a TV script in which I had carefully stated what should appear on screen, the director remarked, 'Your job is to provide the clashes between the characters: I'll take care of the pictures.' The same applies in the theatre.

When reading plays, particularly by writers working in the early years of the century such as Barrie, Shaw, A.A. Milne etc., you may come across such detailed stage directions as:

PETER: *(with a drum beating in his breast as if he were a real boy at last)* To die will be an awfully big adventure.

But these versions were designed almost as novels and intended as far as possible to reproduce the feeling of having been in the theatre at the time of a performance. The script provided for the first production would have been more in the nature of a blueprint for the use of technicians.

Even some old acting editions, without going into such flowery detail, contain more than is strictly necessary with *Sits in chair upstage of sideboard* or *Moves down left to bureau.* This is because they were reprinted from the 'prompt copy' of a West End production. On the prompt copy of a script every detail of a production is recorded – every move, every piece of business, sometimes even inflexions – so that, if necessary, an exact reproduction can be mounted with a different company at another theatre, even in another country.

More recent acting editions include fewer stage directions, so that future generations of actors and directors do not feel tied down to what was in fact only one person's original ideas on the staging of the play.

The setting too should be described in just sufficient detail to enable a designer to start work. In *Peter Pan* Barrie takes two and a half pages to describe the Darling nursery (too long to quote here). Christopher Fry describes the setting for *The Dark is Light Enough* as, *A room with a great staircase,* and for *Venus Observed* as, *A room at the top of a mansion: once a bedroom, now an observatory.* These are two extremes: the ideal lies somewhere between.

If a play is produced in a West End or Broadway theatre, all the resources of modern technology may be available in the shape of lifts, trucks and revolving stages (not to mention lasers). In fact some shows seem to have been conceived merely to exploit their special effects. There have been some spectacular (in every respect) failures because, in spite of fortunes being spent on visual display, the producers had failed to back this up with a worthwhile script.

A playwright whose career has yet to take off is advised to make more modest demands, if only because those early efforts will most likely have their World Première on a small stage with limited facilities. The author in Philip King's *On Monday Next* (about life in a very small theatre) asks for 'a magnificent Adam staircase': he gets the set of three steps 'that we used last week in *Rebecca*'. With the best will in the world the average school or church hall, even when specially converted, will have practical problems in coping with more than one set. Lack of backstage space for storing pieces not in immediate use is often a major headache. It *can* be done, especially by using a basic structure with interchangeable sections and/or furniture. Ingenuity can make a little go a long way; but difficulties in providing a set can be a factor when a company chooses a play.

I have found this from personal experience. My *Everybody's Friend* was awarded The Whitworth Cup for the best one-act play of the year. It was also broadcast and received among others a glowing notice in *The Times*. However it is seldom produced because the setting calls for two old persons' flats side by side. No more furniture is actually needed than for any other modest one-acter – only the arrangement is different to give the illusion of two rooms: but that description of 'two rooms' puts off prospective amateur producers from the start.

There seems to be a growing tendency to write plays with multiple sets, which may be due to the influence of television. Paradoxically many settings may be easier to cope with than just two or three because the design problem has to be approached quite differently. A play can be presented with a curtained surround with just one or two essential items to give an indication of where each scene is taking place. A composite set may be built with different parts of the stage set aside for different locations, for example a living-room at one side of the stage, an office at the other, a pub at the back and a bus stop at the front. An abstract structure such as an arrangement of rostra can indicate various places. The acting editions of my plays *Parcel* and *Who's a Hero, Then?* give stage plans for such settings. The simplest of all is a bare stage, which can be anywhere the writer says it is. (Such as John Godber's *Bouncers*, Thornton Wilder's *Our Town* or my *Life and Death of Almost Everybody*.) If an actor can enter and say with conviction, 'It's cold on these battlements', (or words to that effect) an audience will 'see' those battlements.

Remembering that for the playwright the setting can never be more than background for the action, the best course is to ask for whatever you believe the play requires and hope for the best.

The same applies to lighting, with the added qualification that so many technical advances are being made all the time only a full-time lighting designer is likely to keep up with them. If you want to open a scene by candlelight just before dawn, have daybreak and eventually flood the room with early morning sun, that effect is possible. (I have seen it in a Moscow Arts Theatre production of *Uncle Vanya*.) However if you expect anything approaching that from the Loamshire Thespians performing in the Bishop's Wallop village hall, you are likely to be disappointed. One advantage in knowing for whom you are writing is the chance to adjust to available facilities (while perhaps trying to extend them a little). I once wrote a play for the Scarborough theatre-in-the-round knowing that the stage management would consist of one person to do everything. I arranged matters so that full stage lights came on at the beginning of the play and went off at the end. That was the whole lighting plot. Better safe than sorry.

The last word on stage lighting belongs with Bernard Shaw. Shown a new back-projection device that could produce the appearance of clouds slowly moving across the sky, he congratulated the inventor and hoped to see the device working in the theatre – but not in one of his plays! The sage did not want anything that might distract from his words.

Clever effects can also be achieved through sound. The introduction of the tape recorder (with the more recent addition of the compact disc) has increased the range of possibilities open to the technically minded. Alan Ayckbourn, wearing his director's hat, has always had an ear for a telling suggestion – such as cicadas in his *Man of the Moment*, which fell silent at a sudden noise; or the vampire's last scream in his production of my *Carmilla* which, using four speakers, seemed to spiral round the audience.

The Ghost Train, running since the twenties and still regularly scheduled, owed much of its original success to the effect of an express rushing at full speed outside the station waiting-room in which the action takes place. (Originally achieved in those pre-tape days by a small army of stage staff and not quite so impressive now everyone in the audience knows that it can be done with a flick of a switch.) Somerset Maugham's *Rain* requires a constant background of just that. O'Neill's *The Emperor Jones* requires the continuous and increasing sound of distant drums. However relying too heavily on the efforts of a single back-stage department is risky: if just one thing goes wrong.... What if the train does *not* arrive on time? A production may just survive inept direction and wooden acting, but ill-considered sound effects can wreck a scene, if not a whole play. My *Incident* opens with the sound of an off-stage shower of rain, but I have seen a production in which all the dialogue in the first scene has been literally drowned.

Again ask for what is necessary, but ask yourself first whether or not it is *really* necessary. A sensitive director will be able to pick up and incorporate hints (like Ayckbourn's cicadas); an insensitive director is best kept away from heavy-handed intrusions.

The human voice can also raise problems when it becomes involved with electronics. It can become distorted beyond recognition. Have dialogue coming from a loud-speaker if absolutely necessary, but consider alternatives first.

'Extraordinary how potent cheap music is,' says Amanda in *Private Lives*. Music can add to the atmosphere of a scene. In pre-naturalistic drama it can be used as required – melodrama is literally action accompanied by music – but in a naturalistic play an identifiable source of the sound is advisable. (Such as the off-stage hotel orchestra commented on by Amanda.) Notice that Shakespeare only calls for music in his plays when there are identifiable performers around.

The scenes of a play may be numbered in two ways – what

might be called the English way and the French way.

An English script has the scenes numbered according to changes of time and place. For instance:

Act One Scene One   Deirdre's bedroom. Saturday night.
         Scene Two   Mary's living-room. Next morning.
         Scene Three   The same. Two hours later.

The French way is to change the scene number each time a character enters or leaves. For instance:

Act One   Deirdre's bedroom
                    Scene One – Deirdre, Ron.
                    Scene Two – Deirdre, Ron, Mary.
                    Scene Three – Ron, Mary.
                    Scene Four – Ron.
          Mary's living room
                    Scene Five – Mary.
                    Scene Six – Mary, Ron.
                    Scene Seven – Ron.

Very minor interruptions of the 'Your carriage awaits' order are allowed to happen without a change of scene. (A secretary, for instance, could enter, give a message and exit; but her function would be on a par with the telephone ringing.)

Important note! In the UK or USA a play should never be submitted to a management or publisher set out in this manner.

For a writer though this provides a very convenient way of setting out a detailed scenario (even before adding dialogue) because it is possible to see at a glance who is on stage at any given time, and entrances and exits can be arranged so that the right people are in the right place at the right time.

It helps to avoid the awkwardness of introducing a character, forgetting they are there, and having them hang about with nothing to do. Performers tend to resent this.

It also indicates the number of scenes to an act – in the dramatic sense, not merely as an indication of time and/or place. In an average stage play (other media: other rules) there will be approximately thirty. There may be slightly more in farces and action thrillers in which there tend to be more rapid entrances and exits; fewer in serious drama leaning heavily on serious discussion.

Most importantly though, the playwright should be able to sum up what each scene is about. For instance:

Scene One – Deirdre tries to persuade Ron to run away with her.

Scene Two – Mary expects to find Ron with a sick aunt. Deirdre goes to look for aspirin.

Scene Three – Mary demands an explanation from Ron, and on failing to get it, threatens to divorce him.

Scene Four – Ron rings his aunt inviting her to come on a visit.

A scenario laid out in this way is not compulsory. Different writers have different methods; but I have often found this way useful, if only for being able to see at a glance where, when and how plants and pointers can be slotted into the script. The function of a scene may become more obvious – does it advance the story or is it intended to fill in background, character and/or atmosphere? Or is it needed for transition?

Every French scene should start at point A and progress to point B, at which point the situation will have changed, however slightly. When Eliza first enters the house in Wimpole Street Higgins wants to have her thrown out, but ends by taking her on as a pupil. When Gloucester meets Anne by the coffin she wants to kill him: by the end of the scene she has agreed to marry him. In the first scene of *Victoria Regina* the Duchess of Kent is delighted to hear that the king is dead and she is now the queen's mother: at the end of the scene she is saying, 'What is going to become of me?' If there has been no change, then some rethinking is needed because, no matter how brilliant the dialogue, the play will merely have been marking time.

The scene by scene scenario will also indicate where a different sort of transition is needed – where a character or characters must go off in order that other characters may take the stage.

For example, suppose characters A and B are on stage and in the next major scene a confrontation between characters C and D is needed. A scene break (by lowering and raising curtain or lights) may be undesirable: the action may need to be continuous. A and B could exit, then C and D enter. However this would leave the stage empty with nothing happening. In other words, for no matter how short a time, there would be a hole in the play – time enough for the audience's attention to wander. Never have an empty stage without a very good reason. It is permissible if the attention of the audience has already been directed to something happening off-stage. For instance in *Frankenstein* Clerval is alone in the laboratory destroying vital notes when he hears a noise outside. When he goes to investigate, although the stage is empty the audience is in effect still with him waiting for the inevitable cry and thud. Or the next entrance could be pointed: A could look off-stage, remark, 'Here come C and D. I don't want to meet them'. The pointed imminent arrival of C and D would cover the gap after A and B's exit. The stage may also be empty at the very beginning of a scene, when expectancy rules (Neil Simon's *Chapter Two* and Somerset Maugham's *The Circle* open on empty rooms) or at the very end (as at the curtain of *Journey's End*). Between the beginning and end of a scene though action should be continuous.

So how to exchange A and B with C and D without a hiatus? Obviously some overlap will be needed. The simplest way would be to have C and D enter and have an exchange with A and B, who would then leave. Or C could join A and B, with A then leaving C and B together, and D later entering, after which B leaves. Or any permutation or combination of these characters.

There should never be arbitrary exchanges between such comings and goings. Every scene should have its purpose in the play and not be there merely as a means of transition. It is with this sort of forward planning that an outline with French scenes can be most useful.

Just *how* to get characters on and off the stage is a problem that affects many apprentice (and sometimes quite experienced) playwrights. Characters will enter and exit for two reasons – because the playwright demands that they should, and because they themselves want to. In a good play their comings and goings will be so motivated that they will seem to be perfectly natural and in character. In the not-so-good play the excuse may be so forced that the audience will be aware of the manipulation. (As a Hollywood producer is reputed to have said, 'I smell writers'.) Avoid the outlandish suggestion that draws attention to itself. In *The Second Mrs Tanqueray* Aubrey Tanqueray, about to go out to dinner with some friends, suddenly asks to be excused – so that he can write some letters! In fact Pinero wanted to get him out of the way so that the friends could discuss his forthcoming marriage; but it is a pity he couldn't have come up with a better motive. Even Shakespeare in *The Merry Wives of Windsor* has Mistress Quickly remark, 'Out upon't! What have I forgot?' before hurrying off – and leaving the actress to think of a reason.

The golden rule would seem to be – make the characters *want* to come: make them *want* to go.

If the motive for an entrance or an exit is sufficiently well planted beforehand, no eyebrows will be raised when it happens. To take an example from the sample scenes – if Deirdre were suddenly to ask for an aspirin and go off to look for one, an audience might be forgiven for questioning a rather clumsy piece of stagecraft. If on the other hand she had already been shown to be a nervous type, given to hypochondriacal fluttering, the sudden appearance of her boy-friend's wife in the bedroom might well drive her to the medicine chest. If a character says, 'Where's George? He should have been here half an hour ago', George can walk in with no further explanation.

Entrances are on the whole easier to motivate than exits because people have a good reason for being where they are. Nobody questions a man walking into his own living-room. (These days few would question his walking into someone else's bedroom either.) So the setting can provide a reason for anyone being there. This is probably the reason why so many plays of the twenties and thirties were set in 'A lounge hall in the Home Counties' (complete with staircase) through which everyone had to pass in order to get anywhere. This will also apply to a restaurant, an office, a station waiting-room, etc.

An occasion can do the same – a party, mealtime, meeting....

Sometimes the reason can be an obvious pretext. In her scene with Lopakhin, Varya pretends to have forgotten to pack something. The neighbour in the TV series *Bewitched* was always calling in to borrow a cup of sugar, when the viewer was perfectly aware that the motive was curiosity.

Writers may sometimes be confused by the question of stage time.

All time is relative. If we are enjoying a performance, hours can flash past like minutes. If we are bored, a quarter of an hour can seem a lifetime. Stage time can be even more flexible. In *Saint Joan*, at the end of the trial, she is taken out to be executed. Less than a minute later, 'The glow and flicker of fire can now be seen reddening the May daylight'. There follow a one-minute scene between Cauchon and the Inquisitor, two minutes between Warwick and the Chaplain and a minute between Warwick and Ladvenue – just over five minutes in all. At the end of which the Executioner arrives to announce that nothing remains – 'Not a bone, not a nail, not a hair'. Which is improbable to say the least. An audience accepts the situation without question because there have been six other points to consider within those five minutes. A useful example of an experienced playwright's sleight of hand.

If a character has something to do off-stage, make sure that the interest of the audience is held *on*-stage while that is being done. Failure to manage this is a frequent fault in early scripts. A character will go off – to make tea for instance – and be back with it brewed and ready to pour in thirty seconds while we wait. Gasps of disbelief. If in that same time (plus maybe a few seconds more) the audience had been given something else to think about, that speedy service would have gone unnoticed.

On-stage time can also be speeded up by referring to its passing between peaks of interest. If we are told that something is to happen in half an hour's time, and then in the course of other activity are reminded of the passing of time every three or four minutes, that half-hour can be condensed into ten minutes quite naturalistically. In a non-naturalistic play the problem does not arise: Marlowe's *The Jew of Malta* seems to take place switched to fast-forward.

Linked to time is the serving of stage meals. Unless there is a good reason for their not being eaten, time must be allowed for at least the appearance of this being done. Three classic meals on-stage repay study – tea in *The Importance of Being Earnest*, lunch in the second act of *You Never Can Tell*, and dinner in the second act of *Fallen Angels*. In each of these a full meal is served and apparently enjoyed while the actors continue to talk. Apart from such stage tricks as white bread passed off as fish and brown bread as steak, the writers have tricks of their own.

In the first place the eating is brought into the conversations. 'How can you sit there calmly eating muffins?' demands Jack Worthing at tea. The Waiter at lunch is constantly making suggestions – 'A little more fish, miss?'; 'Salt at your elbow, sir.'; 'Cheese, sir? or would you like a cold sweet?' With a party of seven, as soon as a course has been served to the last member, it is time to clear the plate of the first. No one has any time in which to eat, but constant movement coupled with the Waiter's remarks, creates the illusion of a full meal being consumed quite leisurely in less than ten minutes. With drinks, too. There is a great deal of conspicuous drinking in *Fallen Angels* while the ladies bicker over their meal (drinking is easier to integrate with action). The answer would seem to be – the more the food is talked about, the less need there is to eat it.

For some reason audiences like to see food on-stage. At the very least it gives performers something to do. A piece of general advice might well be: when in doubt, serve a meal. It is sure to hold the attention of the audience.

Getting and holding the attention of an audience has to be the first skill of a playwright. With this knack all other faults will be forgiven; without it the most subtle psychological observation, the most profound thought, even the most dazzling use of language, will go for nothing. This is the reason why some plays, universally praised by the critics for the above qualities, die within days; while others universally disparaged, have run for years.

First catch your audience. As soon as possible. Never forgetting that they are in a theatre.

'Aye, there's the rub.' Whatever the size, shape or form of the theatre, at the opening of the play there will be present a motley collection of all sorts and conditions of people in various stages of readiness. Some will be engaged in conversation that they are reluctant to break off (with people they normally have nothing to say to); some will be struggling out of their coats (they never seem to think of this in the foyer); some latecomers will be pushing past everyone else to get to their seats in the middle of a row (latecomers *always* have seats in the middle of a row); some will already be crinkling the outer wrappings of their boxes of chocolates (others will wait until the actors actually start to speak). They must all be given time to settle down.

Experienced writers will allow anything from one to five minutes for this, during which time nothing of vital importance will happen.

Bearing all that in mind, the playwright has to convert this assembly of disparate persons into the collective being known as an audience – 'The many-headed monster of the pit' (Pope). A tall order. The first step towards this transformation is to unite all those separate entities by rousing their common curiosity.

Fortunately there is usually at least a ten-minute period in which to do this. Very few people walk out in the first ten minutes of a play. Even those who have come to the wrong theatre take some time to realize this. (One man is reputed to have sat through *The Wizard of Oz* under the impression that it was *Macbeth*, on at the theatre next door: both plays have witches.)

The setting, already mentioned, is the first thing to catch attention, especially if it is accompanied by special lighting effects. (Sometimes it will receive a round of applause which, although destructive to atmosphere at least indicates the audience is of a mind about one thing). The cellar of *The Laboratory* is lit by candles and furnace; *Dark of the Moon* opens on top of a mountain with moonlight and fog; my *Singing in the Wilderness* takes place in the sort of wood where one might expect to find fairies. In this opening there may also be sounds of nocturnal wildlife and even a snatch of Mendelssohn's *Midsummer Night's Dream* music and the first thing that happens thereafter is a tinkle of a tiny bell, which seems to dance from bush to bush while a voice off calls, 'Tinkerbell'.

So music and sound can be used effectively. *The Importance of Being Earnest* opens with Algernon playing the piano off-stage. An empty room with a doorbell or telephone ringing has been used more times than can be counted. It may be an overworked device, but it works because the audience is already asking 'Why doesn't somebody answer?' Not only have all those minds been brought together with a mutual query, but the first entrance has been prepared for.

An empty stage (one of the occasions when this is desirable) will have an audience waiting for something to happen on it. Barrie's *Mary Rose* opens on an empty room in an old house, as does my *Winter of 1917*.

Even when there are characters on stage, a pause will have the same effect. At the opening of Peter Ustinov's *The Love of Four Colonels* the colonels sit without speaking for what the author hopes will be the longest pause in theatre history; after which one remarks, 'We seem to have run out of conversation'. In *Arms and the Man* the curtain goes up on Raina standing alone at her bedroom window, a pause which can continue as long as the actress and director consider to be effective. My *Cagebirds* opens with the birds 'totally absorbed in their own thoughts'. The first speech after such a long opening pause will make an audience take notice.

Crowds are fascinated by people doing things – if only by men digging holes. So a piece of business can make a good opening. George in Simon's *Chapter Two* enters and after such preliminaries as turning on the lights and putting down his suitcases, goes through a large quantity of mail 'throwing every second or third piece into the wastebasket'. *The Odd Couple* opens with a member of a poker game slowly and laboriously shuffling a pack of cards. Beth Henley's *Crimes of the Heart* opens with Lennie trying to stick birthday candles into a cookie – fascinating because it can't be done, but she persists. The opposite of a pause: my *In Committee* opens with six members of a committee all talking at once.

An enigmatic fragment of conversation (especially after a pause) makes a good opening. My *Little Brother, Little Sister* opens with a boy and girl in their mid-teens lying on the floor, her head on his chest. After a pause he yawns.

MADAM: My love?

SIR: Hmm?

MADAM: Shhh.

>   (*He sighs. She sighs. He sits up. She sits up.*)

SIR: Play something else.

MADAM: I like this game.

SIR: It makes my head buzz.

All these examples are quite arbitrary, culled from a rapid scan of bookshelves from which dozens of others might just as easily have been chosen. The principles they illustrate will be seen to be contained in almost any successful play.

For an experienced playwright this time spent in focusing the interest of the audience will serve more than one purpose. It will contain plants, even though these may have to be repeated in other ways for the benefit of latecomers; probably contain pointers to the later course of the action; and will also help to set the tone and atmosphere of the play.

Having caught the attention of the audience, the writer's job – the most important and in the last analysis perhaps the only job – is to keep them in their seats and awake.

Avoid monotony.

Necessary variety can be arrived at in the planning stage by contrasting scenes. Try to follow a noisy scene with a quiet one and vice-versa – the way in which the storm of the first scene in *The Tempest* is followed by low-key reminiscence from Prospero, or in *Macbeth* where the horror of the murder of Macduff's family is increased by the quiet family scene preceding it.

Follow fast pace with a gentler tempo. In a comedy do not attempt to be hilarious all the time, but give the audience breathing spaces in which to recover. In his autobiographical *Act One* Moss Hart describes how, on the pre-Broadway tour of *Once in a Lifetime*, audiences stopped laughing two-thirds of the way through each performance; and no amount of rewriting could persuade them to laugh again after that point. After an interval during one of these try-outs Moss Hart found himself talking to a member of the audience who had not bothered to go back for the rest of the show. He protested that it was too noisy. Then the penny dropped. Hart and Kaufman wrote in a new intimate scene that could be played quietly. When that was performed audiences laughed happily to the final curtain. Contrast was the one thing needed.

A romantic sub-plot can provide light relief in more ways than one. Note how the Anne Page/Fenton love passages in *The Merry Wives of Windsor* provide a foil for the knockabout with Falstaff; how in *The Merchant of Venice* an intimate moonlit interlude with Lorenzo and Jessica comes between the business of the rings.

Remember also that in comedy the laughter should increase as the play progresses. Avoid having the funniest scenes at the beginning. The farce writer Feydeau would deliberately remove laughs from early scenes if he thought there were too many. He knew that the pace of a farce has to quicken towards the end, where the longest, loudest laughter should come; and that is achieved by not having it too fast too soon.

This manipulation applies to other types of play besides comedy. Consider the use of contrast between main climaxes. A thriller can be made more effective by lightening the atmosphere before moving in, as it were, for the kill. A really tense situation pursued relentlessly can produce a laugh where a scream was intended. This is because the tension has been wound up too tightly.

Slacken it slightly just before the climax.

In many horror films a false climax is introduced before a real one. Making her way alone up the dark stairs the heroine is startled by a hiss and a shriek – to find that she has stumbled over the cat. A self-deprecatory giggle from both her and the audience relieves the tension so that, when she is suddenly grabbed by the monster, there are real screams from everyone.

Though this technique is seen at its broadest in the horror film (remembering though that the earliest examples, such as *Dracula, The Bat, The Cat and the Canary*, etc. were based on successful stage plays) it can be applied more subtly in the theatre – see the gravediggers' scene in *Hamlet*.

Most classic playwrights seem to have been born knowing all about keeping an audience interested. I doubt if Shakespeare or Shaw read a book on how to do it in their lives. However Shakespeare worked for years in the theatre and Shaw was a dramatic critic. They had seen for themselves what did and did not work with an audience. Shaw said more than once that, at the top of a page, he had no idea of what was going to happen before the bottom. However he did have an instinct that took care of all the above. He himself said that he deliberately constructed his plays like operas with arias, duets, trios, ensembles, etc. In other words there had to be diversity in the composition of his scenes. Morever, in spite of the fact that some of his plays are considered little more than debates, very few Shavian scenes last for longer than five minutes without some interruption or obvious change of direction – from tea being served, to an aviator crashing through the conservatory roof.

After the arrangement of scenes the most direct way of avoiding tedium is through contrast in characters and the way they talk. In other words through the dialogue.

8   Pen to Paper

The spoken word is the mainstay of theatre. Although much can be suggested by what is seen – after all Aristotle included spectacle and music among his elements of drama, and mime and ballet are respected branches of the performing arts – for detail and subtlety speech becomes essential. An accomplished dancer can stir deep emotions and even evoke universal truths, especially when backed by expressive music, but cannot, for instance, inform an audience that he has an aunt in Budleigh Salterton who suspects the retired bookmaker next door of having buried his missing wife in the middle of the rose bed. Deprived of speech, classical ballet devised a complicated language of gesture to signal certain stock phrases such as 'Come', 'Go', 'I love you' etc. (rather like a pocket guide for travellers) but is denied the infinite variety of ways in which the spoken word can be used to convey even those simple messages. (Film and television with their added visual resources – so much can be suggested with a raised eyebrow or the close-up of a tear – must in the end have those pictures backed up by dialogue.)

Unfortunately the minute some would-be playwrights pick up a pen they become afflicted by a sort of amnesia. They forget how to talk. They cannot remember the way they complained to the plumber who failed to turn up on time, the way they asked directions of a passer-by, even the way they proposed: and the way in which all those others replied. Instead what emerges is as formal as an application for an overdraft or a schoolboy translation from a dead language.

This lapse is brought on mainly by the unnatural

posture of sitting in front of a blank sheet of paper instead of murmuring into a telephone or shouting across a counter. When a play is being written, all the parts are in effect being acted first inside the writers' head. But when the writer is sitting in front of that paper, instead of such roles as 'fond lover' or 'outraged customer', the only part being played is that of 'a writer'. The way out of this is to move from posing into being. When faced with the tools of the trade try thinking of yourself not so much as a writer as a member of the human race. (If it is of any consolation, I frequently find myself writing first drafts on the backs of envelopes, bill, circulars, any sort of scrap paper – just to convince my subconscious that I am not actually writing.) Ask yourself, 'What would I really say in this situation?' Later it will be necessary to progress to what a particular character would say, but at least it is a beginning, and almost any first draft can be improved by rewriting.

'Ping-pong' dialogue is probably the easiest to write. In this style character A says a line, then B responds in such a way that the end of the speech acts as a cue for A again. A replies, giving the next cue for B. And so on. Something like this exchange from my *En Attendant François*:

MAVIS: Tonight's night out seemed to lack something that a night out ought to have.

ROSE: My fault again, I suppose.

MAVIS: You did ask me to come.

ROSE: My mistake.

MAVIS: You said, 'Make up a foursome, Mavis'. If you didn't want me, why did you ask me?

ROSE: Because you were the first one I thought of.

MAVIS: That's nice, Rose. Couldn't you really think of anybody else?

ROSE: Why else do you think I asked you?

MAVIS: That isn't quite so nice.

Actors like this sort of dialogue because learning is easier when one line suggests the next. But it can become boring for the listener. If all the speeches in a play are about the same length and have the same rhythm, the result can be hypnotic – and the last thing any playwright wants is to put the audience to sleep. So try to vary the dialogue.

Personally I examine the content of each scene and consider which of the many sorts of dialogue might best convey the mood I am trying to establish. Unless otherwise stated the following excerpts are all from Campton plays – not blowing my own trumpet but because I know what I was trying to do when I wrote them.

Very short speeches – sometimes even monosyllables – flashing between the characters might be best for an interrogation, a quarrel or panic. As from *Memento Mori*:

YOUNG MAN: The sanitation?

OLD MAN: Crumbling, but restorable.

YOUNG MAN: The roof?

OLD MAN: Very few leaks.

YOUNG MAN: Dry rot?

OLD MAN: Hardly a trace.

YOUNG MAN: The paint?

OLD MAN: Peeled.

YOUNG MAN: That's honest. The drive?

OLD MAN: Pits and potholes.

YOUNG MAN: Discourages visitors.

OLD MAN: A load of gravel works wonders.

YOUNG MAN: Or a little earth.

OLD MAN: For charity.

Or from *Split Down the Middle*:

JOSIE: *(shouting)* Help!

FRAN: *(shouting)* Help!

JOSIE: Do you think anybody heard us?

FRAN: They didn't reply.

JOSIE: They weren't listening.

FRAN: Who?

JOSIE: Anybody. *(shouting)* Help!

FRAN: *(shouting)* Help!

JOSIE: Can you see anything?

FRAN: Only the fog.

JOSIE: It's not a fog. *(shouting)* Help!

FRAN: *(shouting)* It looks like a fog.

JOSIE: It's a fret.

Short speeches with pauses between could establish the romantic feeling of a love scene, as in 'Darling' ... (Pause) ... 'What, darling?' ... (Pause) ... 'Just – (Pause) – darling, darling.' Or embarrassment as in *Then*:

PHYTHICK: Ridiculous.

(Pause.)

GIRL: Silly.

                        (Pause.)

PHYTHICK: For one minute....

                        (Pause.)

GIRL: I thought so too.

                        (Pause.)

PHYTHICK: That I was making love to a brown paper
               bag.

                        (Pause.)

GIRL: It's a good bag.

Long uninterrupted speeches can be used to advance an argument or justify a point of view. The Inquisitor's speech summing up in *Saint Joan* goes on for several pages. Rather shorter in *Reserved*:

WAITRESS: Crying never changed circumstances. In
               fifteen years one learns to adapt to circum-
               stances: the bed-sit with the one-bar, the
               forty-watt bulb and the bathroom down the
               passage – 'Please leave as you would hope to
               find' but one never finds what one hopes;
               the daily bus with the standing-room-only
               except on days when it doesn't stop at all;
               the little economies to pay for the little
               luxuries that seem to make the little econo-
               mies pinch ever tighter. Still one doesn't cry.
               One doesn't even complain. Who is there to
               complain to? What is there to complain
               about? Who is to blame for the past fifteen
               years?

What is in fact a long speech, punctuated by short interruptions, may heighten an accusation, defence or cross-examination as in Rattigan's *The Winslow Boy*. Or *Reserved*:

WAITRESS: Don't tempt me.

SHOPPER: Why not?

WAITRESS: One has been tempted. I'll admit that. From time to time. One can be tempted when confronted by the lowest of the low.

SHOPPER: Such as?

WAITRESS: The slip and slop brigade.

SHOPPER: Oh, yes.

WAITRESS: By the sliced bread and packet soup lot.

SHOPPER: Yes, yes.

WAITRESS: The 'Where's the tomato sauce?' crowd, who give their order as though to equals. If only they knew.

SHOPPER: Oh, yes, yes, yes.

WAITRESS: One is tempted, but one learns control. One's training carries one through. One says 'Yes, madam' and 'Thank you, madam.'

SHOPPER: You do.

WAITRESS: But one leaves no doubt as to who is in control.

A series of longer speeches can create the right setting for reminiscence; especially if the speeches follow characters' individual thoughts instead of being in reply to one another. Again from *Reserved*:

SHOPPER: I know what you're doing. I've brought up six of my own, so I ought to know. You're playing on my sympathies. That's what you're doing. I've had my sympathies played on before now, you know.

WAITRESS: One has never asked for sympathy. No matter how much one needed it. One wouldn't have got it anyway.

SHOPPER: Six of your own are always playing on your sympathies. With six of your own you need the fun-size sympathy pack, I can tell you.

WAITRESS: One learns to live without.

SHOPPER: No half-past closing time.

WAITRESS: I had a mother for a little while. I remember she'd put her arms around me while I cried softly against her bosom. Once upon a time.

SHOPPER: Me – I brought up six of my own.

WAITRESS: Then one grew up. One stopped crying. Even when one's toys were lost. All of them. The tiny tea service and the rag dolls. One forgot that one ever had rag dolls to wait on with the tiny toy tea service. One waited at table here instead.

You will have seen that it is not essential that every speech should be in response to the one immediately previous to it. People do not necessarily talk like that. Often they will pursue their own train of ideas, or suddenly respond to a point made some time previously. Try to follow that line of thought as in this passage from *Silence on the Battlefield*:

BRENDA: We must find a way to leave in peace without making life hell.

LILLY: I'll make the tea when Coral comes. Or when you feel thirsty, whatever suits you. Now what else do we want? Oh, silly-billy. Cups, saucers and plates.

BRENDA: We must have rules.

LILLY: I suppose we couldn't have the best cups? No, better not.

BRENDA: We must each know what is expected of us, and just what each can expect from the others.

LILLY: I don't expect Coral will be long now.

BRENDA: We must have rules, and know them, and stick to them.

LILLY: I should have liked some celery. Crisp, fresh celery, with a sprinkle of salt to go with my bread and butter. And cheese, of course.

BRENDA: Will – you – listen to me?

LILLY: I have been listening.

The *action* of the scene though should still proceed as directly as possible from point A to point B.

Incidentally such expressions as 'by the way' or 'that reminds me' are danger signals, often indicating that somewhere the argument has run off the rails and needs to be brought back into line. Instead of 'by the way ...' analyse the earlier part of the scene to find out where the information really should have gone.

Try also to use concrete rather than abstract expressions. 'Nice day' is all very well, but 'Hot enough for you?' or 'Call this flaming June?' carries the idea a step further. 'You're going to be late' is a simple statement; 'If you don't get a move on, you're going to miss that train,' has an added dimension.

In addition to conveying information and mood, dialogue is also an active ingredient in characterization. Speech patterns and the use of words are almost as individual as fingerprints. An elderly university professor is not likely to talk in the same way as a teenage shop girl, nor a star actress like a punch-drunk boxer. Not only will their vocabulary and expressions be different, but so will their speech rhythms. Occupation, education, birthplace, domicile, age, etc., all have an effect. There is as much difference between the speech rhythms of a motor mechanic and a clergyman as between a Welshman and an American from the Deep South.

A warning though about the use of slang and swearing.

Slang can date a play more quickly than the costumes the performers are wearing. Slang is part of a living language, and can sometimes be incorporated into it. Usually though its life is very short – by the time an expression reaches print it is likely to be on its way out. This use-by date (itself a colloquial expression) is reached even faster by the young: by the time an adult can understand what they are talking about, a new set of expressions is in vogue.

Handled *very* carefully – so easy to get the exact use wrong – it can provide background detail for a period piece: 'masher,' 'knut', 'old fruit', 'flannel', 'gone for a Burton' all precisely indicate their periods.

Bad language needs even more care in its handling. Although taboos are less rigid than they were when Eliza's 'bloody' sent shock waves through the theatre, potential audiences must be considered. Marketing here comes into the equation – and will be further considered when the time comes to sell the play. Remember that a word likely to pass unnoticed in a London fringe production is equally likely to outrage the audience of a rural drama group (even supposing it were likely to get as far as a production in the church hall, which is unlikely).

Sometimes its use is unavoidable. A not-too-bright member of an East End gang is hardly likely to say 'tut' or 'bother' (unless as part of deliberate characterization). In that context swearing may be acceptable. In situations where there is no alternative, go ahead – while remembering that part of the audience will react (even over-react) to blasphemy or obscenity and inevitably be alienated. Artistic integrity is to be respected, but in the theatre it is the audience that pays the bills.

In Waterhouse and Hall's *Billy Liar* the father uses the word 'bloody' so often that it becomes meaningless, except as a characterizing trait. Repetition can have that effect. It is a useful adjunct in the writing of dialogue. To

Myrtle in Paul Osborn's *Morning's at Seven* everything about Homer's backyard is 'heavenly'.

Dickens (one of the best writers of dialogue the theatre never had) repeatedly used the repetition of a word or phrase – Heep's "umble', Micawber's waiting for 'something to turn up', Sam Weller's 'As the . . . . said'. However the device must be used with discretion – overdone (as in ITMA's 'Can I do you now, sir?') it belongs to the world of farce and sit. com.

This way of picking up and repeating a word or phrase not only stresses the expression, but can effectively integrate it into the rhythm of a scene. Such as:

'I'm going to Manchester.'

'Manchester, eh?'

'Yes, Manchester.'

'So you're going to Manchester, are you?'

'Are *you* going to Manchester?'

'Why should I want to go to Manchester? Never been to Manchester. Why should I go to Manchester now?'

Notice that, although the above may be a dialogue between two Northerners (or Cornishmen or Welshmen) it is written in accepted English. Do not try to reproduce accents phonetically on the page. Here are two quotations: From Harold Brighouse's *Lonesome Like*: 'Ah thowt A'd mebbe a chance wi' yon lass as were 'ere wi' thee, but hoo towld me A were too late.' And from Shaw's *Captain Brassbound's Conversion*: 'Waw, it's the nime is blessed mather give im at er knee! Ther ynt noaw awm in it.' One was written by a native of Lancashire, the other is a Dubliner's idea of Cockney. What they have in common is that they are equally infuriating to sight read. Believe it or not, actors are actually trained to speak in dialect. (Some are better at it than others, just as some can fence better than others – to each his own talents.) Just indicate to them what dialect is required and trust to their skills for the effect you want. For instance if your character is a drunken Glaswegian, it is sufficient to note the fact, then write the lines in conventional English. Do not ever pepper the pages with apostrophes to indicate dropped aitches or gees: they merely give the reader (who may not even be an actor) the double task of having to translate before coming to terms with your lines.

The great disadvantage the theatre suffers when compared with the novel is that the audience's perception is limited to what is seen and heard. There is no way in which the audience can get inside a character's head, to be sure of what is happening in his mind in as simple a way as the storyteller writing 'He thought'. Barrie can write:

SIR HARRY: (remembering perhaps a rectory garden)....

But as Sir Harry fails to mention that rectory garden, the audience knows nothing about it.

Over the years playwrights and audiences have agreed on certain conventions to deal with the problem.

In the beginning was The Chorus, which filled in the audience on what was happening between the lines. Anouilh retains this character in his adaptation of the Greek *Antigone*. More recently, in Thornton Wilder's *Our Town*, the name was changed to The Stage Manager, but the function remained the same. In some plays the character is simply called The Narrator. Sometimes this character also takes part in the play. Tom Jones does it in Joan Macalpine's adaptation of Fielding's novel. Dolly Levi does it in Wilder's *The Matchmaker*. Tom does it in Tennessee Williams's *The Glass Menagerie*. If this convention is to be used, try to establish it as soon as possible so that it becomes part of the contract with the audience. An audience will accept any convention if it is agreed early enough and is kept up.

From the Chorus/Narrator there is only a small step to the soliloquy. This allows a character to speak thoughts, though not necessarily directly to the audience. In Hamlet's 'To be or not to be' soliloquy he is unburdening himself with the assumption that he is *not* being overheard. The audience is allowed to eavesdrop. A few centuries later in Pinero's *The Magistrate* Mr Posket relives his flight and pursuit from a shady hotel. He is alone in his office behind the courtroom and, since he is admitting to breaking the law and evading arrest, the presumption again must be that he is not overheard.

Between the convention of direct address by a narrator

and the soliliquy comes the aside. An aside is usually shorter than a soliloquy. It is sometimes used like a soliloquy as thoughts revealed; and it is sometimes addressed to the audience, openly acknowledging that they are there. This convention is frequently used in burlesque melodrama, making fun of a practice that little more than a hundred years ago was accepted quite seriously. Its use depends on acknowledging from the opening of the play that there is an audience present and that it is included in the action. There is a sequence of asides in my *Ragerbo*:

MRS MAMMON: Every time you come round you ask to see the books. It's not as if you could read. Don't you trust me?

RAGERBO:　　　I don't even trust myself.

MRS MAMMON: Trust you!

(She retires behind the clothes rack.)

RAGERBO:　　　As a matter of fact, I can read the books as well as she can. But if I pretend I can't, I stand a better chance of catching her out if she tries it on. Thinking I can't read, she'll be careless.

(MRS MAMMON *puts her head round the rail*)

MRS MAMMON: As a matter of fact I know he can read the books as well as I can. If I were trying anything on, it wouldn't go through the books.

(She withdraws)

RAGERBO:　　　As a matter of fact, I know that she knows I can read the books as well as she can. But if she sees this little trap, she'll walk careful in case of others that she can't see.

(MRS MAMMON *returns with a large ledger*.)

MRS MAMMON: As a matter of fact ... but why should I
    put you wise to everything?

In this play Ragerbo makes his first entrance through
the audience, haranguing them as he does so. The
relationship between the two is established from the start.

On TV, Rumpole has a way of muttering asides which
change when he is asked to repeat them. This is only
really credible in a medium where the listener can catch
the softest whisper. It can be used on-stage, but only in
the broadest comedy. Voice Over (the unseen narrator or
thought spoken without the performer's mouth being
opened) is also regularly used in film and TV.

The arrival of the convention of the fourth wall brought
to the stage previously unknown difficulties for the writer.
People do not usually walk around talking to themselves
(unless that peculiarity has been made part of their
character: which has been done, but cannot be done too
often). Some ingenious tricks have been tried. In *Mr
Sampson* one of the characters talks to a grandfather clock.
Pets can be useful. In John Van Druten's *Bell, Book and
Candle* the witch heroine, Gillian, talks to her cat
Pyewacket. In Frederick Lonsdale's *Canaries Sometimes
Sing* a character talks to her bird. Recently the tape
recorder (like its predecessor the dictaphone) has
provided a lifeline: but this has become something of a
cliché (which means use it if you must, but try to find a
different way of using it.)

There is also a related problem in revealing something
that has been written. People do not usually read aloud. 'I
can't find my glasses, will you please tell me what this
says,' has been done to death. And one trouble with
ingenuity is that it can draw undesirable attention to itself.

One final solution would seem to be: make a virtue of
necessity. Say in effect, 'All right, we know people don't
really speak their thoughts, but let's suppose they do'.
O'Neill did this in *Strange Interlude*. Unfortunately in that
case the running time of the play was doubled.

What cannot be said aloud in a naturalistic play must be
implied. If a situation is made absolutely clear to an
audience in the first place, the dialogue can develop

beyond basic explanation. More than one thing can be happening at the same time. In the last act of *The Cherry Orchard* there is a scene between Varya and Lopakhin. From all that has gone before the audience knows that he wants to marry her and she wants him to ask her. But he cannot bring himself to raise the subject and she cannot prompt him. So they talk about such trivialities as packing and the weather while, from what has led up to the situation, the audience is aware of what they must be thinking. In the second act of Coward's *Present Laughter* Gary and Joanna make love on the settee while comparing the acoustics of concert halls. In these instances the fact that the characters are doing something at variance to what they are saying adds a further dimension to the play.

This underlying, unstated action is sometimes known as sub-text. In light comedy it can be very slight; in a lot of work by Harold Pinter, Terence Rattigan and Jean-Jacques Bernard for instance the sub-text is more important than the main text. However it is present to some extent in most plays.

Always aim for truth in dialogue. Ask (not necessarily at the time of writing when in full flow, but certainly in revision), 'Would such a person in such a situation really have said this?' If the answer is 'no', then no matter how funny or apparently effective, the line must be changed. One of the hardest lessons to grasp – especially for a young playwright full of ideas – is that the best joke in the world when out of place is a dead weight. Be prepared to cut ruthlessly.

When the writing is not progressing as quickly or as smoothly as you would like, there is a great temptation to push a character aside and do the talking for them. This happens particularly when there is a difficult point of the plot to be got over, or you suspect the audience may not be getting the message. The result is invariably wooden and unconvincing. Always let the characters speak for themselves, even if this means taking more time and thought. (John Galsworthy – of *The Forsyte Saga, Strife*, etc. is reputed to have waited for hours, pen in hand, for a character to utter the next speech.)

Characters make a story. They are the one element a

play cannot do without. A short story may be purely descriptive (try some of Virginia Woolf's, such as *Street Haunting*). A play is a different matter because although a bad play can be presented with a defective story-line – or even no perceptible story-line at all – with the critics dismissing it and audiences walking out, at least it *can* go on. Whereas if there is nobody on stage, the audience has nothing with which it can make contact. No matter how crude or inadequately drawn they may be, you must have characters. So how are they to be created?

The only place from which characters can come is inside the author. This applies even with historical characters. The lead in *The Man of Destiny* is not the real-life Napoleon, but Shaw's recreation, with more of Shaw in him than the historical Bonaparte. A play is in effect acted out with all the parts performed in the author's mind, and the result committed to paper. Just as anyone can write dialogue of a sort because anyone can talk, so anyone can create characters because everyone has a sort of repertory company inside them. You may not realize who they are until you start to write, and then you may be surprised – pleasantly or otherwise (creative writing can be very revealing). Dr Jekyll and Mr Hyde is more than mere literary fantasy.

The educationalist Bruner in his work *Creative Thinking* noted that there is within each person a cast of characters – which may in fact be opposites – an ascetic and perhaps a glutton, a prig, a frightened child, a little man, a know-it-all.... He could have gone on to include a bully, a gentle soul, a sophisticate, a coward. Only you will really know, and then probably only after looking back over a series of plays. A number of mine, especially those with all female dramatis personae, seem to have been devised for a single Women's Institute or Townswomen's Guild (though they weren't). All the characters are different, yet a group of six able to stage one of these plays would be able to cast all the others.

Some writers have a very large internal company. Shakespeare leaps to mind as one whose basic cast seems infinite. Yet after a little thought you will realize that this is not so. Julia, Viola and Rosalind have more in common than the fact that they are all girls who dress as boys (to be played by boys dressed as girls). Iago and Iachimo have more in common than the likeness of their names. Slender in *The Merry Wives of Windsor* comes from the same mould as Sir Andrew Aguecheek in *Twelfth Night*. Other writers do very well with a much smaller basic company – look at Coward, Wodehouse or Ben Travers.

The ability to devise a great variety of characters is an asset, but by no means vital. A playwright may have other compensating talents.

So what must writers do to create from this basic repertory company? They change the detail on the types. Falstaff has a lot in common with Sir Toby Belch, but they are no more alike than the two young lovers Lorenzo and Romeo.

The list of absolutely basic types is strictly finite anyway. There are not so many archetypes from which all others are derived. Think of a few in their various manifestations....

The figure of authority: the father figure (who may be the mother figure) inevitably played by a Heavy Character actor in the old stock company, and ranging through world drama from Creon in *Antigone* via Lear to Mr Spettigue in *Charley's Aunt*. Priests, doctors, judges, policemen, bosses of either sex come into this category.

The simple soul: who may be anything from the traditional youngest son in a fairy story to Mr Magoo or Billie Dawn in *Born Yesterday*. A recurring character in Alan Ayckbourn's plays is the innocent who wanders, blissfully ignorant, through a minefield of explosive human relationships.

The mischief maker: this was The Vice in Medieval drama, standing in for The Devil (who occasionally appeared in person). He turns up in many guises – Puck, Iago, Harlequin, Scapin, or whatever character Groucho Marx may have been playing in his films. This is the character who delights in stirring things up.

The loser: romantically wistful like Pierrot, baffled like the magistrate, Mr Poskett, inadvisedly optimistic like Charley Brown, tragic like Willy Loman – everything this character touches seems to fall apart. (Though he is sometimes rewarded by getting the girl, especially in old film comedies.)

The survivor: who made one of his first appearances as Homer's Ulysses, but who has become more in evidence lately. An example in the drama of the thirties was Regina Giddens in Lillian Hellman's *The Little Foxes*. This archetype will lie, cheat, even kill to survive – a trait that seems to strike a chord with modern audiences. Think of the hero of almost any recent melodrama, think of James Bond or Scarlett O'Hara.

The detective: he (or she) tends to stand slightly aside from the main action, sorting through the tangled strands of the story and usually tying them into a neat bow at the end. He becomes more involved in the outcome when his name happens to be Oedipus or Hamlet. Obvious names may already have occurred to you but, as with the two just mentioned, the character need not appear in a conventional whodunit. In J.B. Priestley's *Dangerous Corner* Robert Caplan determinedly pursues the truth about his family; Dr Livingstone in John Pielmeier's *Agnes of God* tries to unravel the circumstances surrounding a young nun's killing of her baby.

The scapegoat: a type most used in melodrama and horror. Dracula, Mr Hyde, Frankenstein's creation, Sweeney Todd and even rather less monstrous villains fall into this category. Their purpose is to draw on to themselves feelings of terror and revulsion so that at the end of the play, when they are killed off, everyone in the audience can feel comfortably safe.

You may be able to think of more, though I doubt whether there will be many.

Basic types have served as a starting point for character since Greek and Roman actors first put on characteristic comic and tragic masks. In the Middle Ages and early Tudor times plays were given casts of abstract qualities: appearing with Everyman in the play of that name are Good Deeds, Friendship, Goods, Knowledge, etc. Ben Jonson thought of his characters in terms of 'humours' or predominant traits – cunning, avaricious, optimistic, lecherous, silly, etc. In his play *Volpone* the characters are named (in Italian) after animals – fox, fly, vulture, parrot.

The Italian *commedia dell'arte* was improvised drama in which the same characters appeared again and again – Harlequin, Columbine, Pantaloon, Doctor, Captain: a tradition that lingers in present-day pantomime with its Principal Boy, Principal Girl, Dame, Broker's Men and all. Nineteenth-century barnstorming melodrama had its hero, heroine, old father, villain. The tradition was taken up by Hollywood and has been continued in such film genres as the Western (villain in black hat, hero in white), Cops and Robbers (with its straight lead, contrasting sidekick, disapproving figure of authority and Aunt Sally villain) and Horror (with grotesque monster relentlessly pursuing heroine, at least one disbelieving figure of authority, hero and optional mad scientist). Hollywood does what writers down the centuries have done – takes types and changes the detail.

It is detail that changes types into people. Note how Shaw does it in *The Devil's Disciple*. He turns the colourless character of the hero of conventional melodrama upside down. The conventional hero is too good to be true and loves his aged parents: Dick Dudgeon is a free-thinking reprobate who cannot stand the sight of his mother. Shakespeare (sorry to keep bringing him up but, still going strong after three centuries, he can still be relied upon to provide an example) took an old revenge tragedy and by adding detail to the characters turned it into the *Hamlet* we know today. It is detail that will change an insipid juvenile or cardboard villain into a real person.

A game used in writing workshops is to go round a circle asking each member in turn to contribute a characterizing detail, starting with such pro forma items as age, sex, address, job, family, interests and then, as a picture begins to emerge, adding more relevant details usually suggested by what has gone before. Depending on the size of the circle, by the time the questioning has been round two or three times, a distinctive person will have emerged, with the suggestion of a story already beginning to form around them. The value of having other players in the game lies in the way other minds can add diversity – so that, for instance, a ten-year-old rag and bone merchant who is saving to buy a piano is already on the way to independent existence. Even when alone though the technique can be applied to existing (if nebulous) characters. Suppose your detective is at first sight an undistinguished questioning machine. What difference will it make if he/she (and consider gender for a start) is Chinese, Jewish, Indian, Belgian, Irish, Australian? Is he/she single, married, divorced, working class, middle class, or aristocrat? What about hobbies – riding, music, drinking, gambling, embroidery? Another help towards developing a three-dimensional character is to include some detail in contrast to the main outline. Authoritarian, homicidal Cook in *Little Brother, Little Sister* cherishes fond memories of the long-dead Bert; Sherlock Holmes plays the violin (though the music-loving villain is now a bit of a cliché).

However there is a certain risk in going into *too much* detail before the character is actually involved in action. Such detail may not only be arbitrary, but lead in a wrong direction. Also there is a temptation, knowing such details, of dragging them in, no matter how superfluous they may be. If you have written a full biography of a character which includes the information that he worked for five years in a biscuit factory, no matter how irrelevant that fact may be, you may find that biscuit factory assuming a disproportionate influence. When I was much younger a tutor, commenting on an outline I had submitted, insisted that I should have given much more detail on the background of a leading character. For instance what did the chap do on his afternoons off? Did he spend them in the cinema, the library, or did he go swimming? Being inexperienced I was rather thrown. Today I would have replied that, in the context of the play, what the chap did on his afternoons off didn't matter a hoot; but if the question should arise in the course of the action then he would tell me without prompting. John Van Druten in his *Playwright at Work* suggested that the author should be able to answer questions about anything concerning his characters, but that he should not have consciously thought it out.

The fact is, the better you get to know your characters, the more details will emerge of their own accord. Ibsen is on record as remarking that the process of getting to know his characters could be slow and painful. As a rule his plays had three casts, which differed considerably from each other (though in detail of character, not in the progress of the story). When he first settled down to work on his material he felt as though he was getting to know the characters as though they were on a railway journey, having just become acquainted and striking up a conversation, chatting about this and that. When he rewrote, he began to see everything more clearly. Then he knew the people as well as if he had been staying with them on holiday for a month. He had got to know the main points of their characters and their little peculiarities.

I would go further than that and say that not only should you know your characters as well as you know your own friends but, like your friends, they should be capable of taking you by surprise. That is constantly happening to me. I had no idea until half-way through *Incident* that the heroine's friend would suddenly turn on her for refusing to accept a room in the hotel annexe; until she revealed the fact I had no inkling that Gianetta da Brescia in *The Laboratory* had poisoned her first husband (or even that she'd had a previous husband); or when she first appeared that Aunt Harriet in *The Life and Death of Almost Everybody* was really The Devil. That is part of the magic of writing.

What characters *are* is inextricably linked to what they *do*: they do such things because of who they are. The plot versus character debate ('Which is the more important? – Discuss') is irrelevant. The situation in which a character may be placed may be something over which he or she has no control, but what he or she *is* will affect the way in which he/she reacts to it, and so decides the future course of events. Imagine what might have happened if Romeo and Hamlet had found themselves in each other's plays. Hamlet would have dithered until Juliet had married Paris – result no tragedy. Sometimes a character must be created to lead to the ending required by the playwright, even though that may seem like working backwards. Unless Ibsen had given Nora the necessary streak of toughness, she would never have walked out on her husband. If

Arthur Miller's John Proctor had not been so weak as to have an affair with his servant yet strong enough to defy the witch hunters, *The Crucible* would have had a different ending. In the course of writing, though, these characters became living people.

Sometimes that depth of characterization is not required. In fact, depending on the sort of play, it could actually be harmful. A farce or detective thriller is likely to work better with natural-seeming puppets than with real people. Audiences can laugh at a character losing his trousers or slipping on a banana skin in a farce because he is a two-dimensional character, whereas a real person in that predicament might generate sympathy. The same applies to the Miss Scarlet, Professor Plum, Rev Black, Cluedo-type characters of the whodunit. What is on display in those instances is the writer's dexterity – akin to juggling or pulling rabbits out of a hat.

Nor should audiences be allowed to become too involved with minor characters. It is one thing to give a small-part actor something to do (you will be thanked for it) but be careful not to become so fascinated with the character that it takes attention away from the leads. If you should find a character growing in this way, save him/her for another play.

I once ran into trouble over a small part in a full-length play that was bought, rehearsed and tried out for the West End (but died before getting there). I brought in a fresh character for the last scene (so the part was bound to be small). I wanted that scene to be the funniest in the play, so becoming the memory audiences would be bound to take away with them: I wanted them to leave the theatre laughing. In that I succeeded. I believe if the play had reached Shaftesbury Avenue the career of the actress would have received a major boost; *but* the attitude of the rest of the cast tended to be 'We've been slogging away for two hours, then she comes on and takes all the applause – not to mention the best notices'. The point had not occurred to me at the play's first production in a provincial theatre, because there the company had been acting as a group and the total effect was all that counted. On the way to London, though, commercial considerations, not to mention the 'star system', raised their heads. The part was not rewritten, but in the latter stages of rehearsal the director was deliberately playing down those laughs. That was not the sole reason why the option on the play was not taken up, but it was a lesson on writing small parts.

Also make sure that every one of your minor characters is really necessary. Remember that each will require a person on stage, which in the professional theatre will mean another pay packet – with its consequential increase in the cost of putting on the play. Even in the amateur theatre the size of the cast can be a consideration. More importantly for the success of a play, one well-drawn character is more effective than two merely sketched in.

This was brought home to me when I adapted Sheridan Le Fanu's *Carmilla* for the Scarborough theatre-in-the-round. After being advised of the size of the available company I prepared a scene by scene scenario; only to be told that a budget revision meant that I would have two fewer bodies. Accordingly I incorporated the part of a maid in with that of the governess, and instead of having two characters as hero and mountebank (essential to the story but with only two brief appearances) had the hero appear *disguised* as a mountebank. The story-line was actually strengthened by these condensations because a closer relationship was established between the heroine and the governess; while the scenes between Carmilla and the mountebank, instead of being chance encounters, became part of the hero's plan to protect the heroine from the vampire.

Always check that you are not using two characters to do what one might be doing better.

You might even come to the conclusion that a character might be more effective if he/she never actually appears. Off-stage characters have a way of enriching a cast at no extra cost to the management. Perhaps the most famous is Mrs Grundy, repeatedly referred to in Tom Morton's eighteenth-century comedy *Speed the Plough* and who, in spite of never being seen, makes such an impact that she has entered the language as the embodiment of a censorious neighbour. Mrs de Pass, the head witch, in Van Druten's *Bell, Book and Candle* and the next-door air hostesses in Neil Simon's *Prisoner of Second Avenue* are just two modern examples. There are many others.

Linked to the economical use of characters is the problem of the small part demanding special skills or attributes. In the professional theatre those attributes must be paid for. To take an obvious example, if a character were required to juggle with oranges while reciting 'The Charge of the Light Brigade', a casting agency would no doubt be able to suggest several of its clients *but* the pay required would be several times that of the usual small-part actor. To take a less obvious example, you might have written in a part demanding outstanding charm and/or personal magnetism: star quality in fact. But stars demand star billing and star salaries. Even if one could be found to take on a small part, the management would not be able to afford it. This problem also extends to writing small but difficult parts for middle-aged to elderly performers. Natural wastage in the profession means that performers over fifty are either reaching the top (and so requiring top pay) or the fact that they are never likely to reach the top is only too obvious. This restriction does not apply in the amateur theatre where some of the most experienced players are delighted to be offered parts that give the chance to perform without making too many demands on stamina or memory.

A cliché of the theatre is, 'Never perform with children or dogs', if only because while they are on stage the audience tends to look at little else. In the professional theatre a child is allowed to give only a certain number of consecutive performances, which necessitates duplication in casting, and a child performer must always have a chaperone, which also adds to the cost. Child actors are not to be ruled out entirely, but be aware of the difficulties that such a part may raise.

Finally, most characters are incomplete without a name. Ideally the name should add something to the character without being too obvious. The habit in earlier drama of hanging on to characters such labels as Sir John Brute, Squire Sullen, Mr Pinchwife, Fainall, Lady Sneerwell has now passed. It is advisable only in non-naturalistic plays: the 'hero' nonentity of Elmer Rice's expressionist *The*

Adding Machine is Mr Zero, and two characters in J.B. Priestley's *Johnson Over Jordan* are Sir James Porker and Madame Vulture. Dickens at his best had a way of evoking character through a name – Murdstone, Squeers, Scrooge, Guppy, Heep.... Henry James (another novelist who aspired to the stage, but who never quite made it) would list names in a notebook as they occurred to him, so that when a character needed to be christened there was a choice waiting.

I do this myself to some extent. Sometimes the name itself will suggest a character. *Mrs Meadowsweet* grew from the name: from the moment it flickered into my mind I knew that she was going to be really nasty in a charming sort of way.

Names seem to affect the conduct of characters. I cannot imagine a Tracey behaving like a Henrietta or a Dick like a Jasper. Some writers find that they cannot make a start until they know the names of their characters. Some have discovered half-way through that the original name was wrong, that their Fred Socks refused to talk like a Lionel de Vere, and have to rename the character from the beginning.

Personally I prefer characters to tell me what their names are, which they usually do after two or three pages, and I am quite prepared to call them A B and C until then. This system seems to work for me, but I can well understand it being impossible for others. Everyone has to find their own way of writing.

Strange but true department: no matter how outlandish the name you invent may be, the odds are that someone somewhere will have it. The laws of libel being what they are, it is inadvisable to have a really unpleasant character with an uncommon name. If your Hilary Navelclough of Newton le Willows is a Chartered Accountant, and is not only embezzling funds but having an affair with his daughter-in-law, another Chartered Accountant from Chester-le-Street, who also happens to be named Hilary Navelclough, might get the idea that you are holding him up to hatred, ridicule or contempt. (Sorry, Mr Navelclough – wherever you are.) Smith, Jones or Robinson is much safer for a villain. There may be many dubious persons around named Brown, White or Green, but they can hardly claim that you specially singled them out.

Finally (unless there is a very good reason – as with Pinky and Perky) avoid characters with names that are too similar. Douglas and Dougal, Betty and Betsey, Conan and Cohan, Wilkins and Wilson. Such soundalikes tend to confuse an audience, which is never a good idea.

9 Special Considerations

All that has gone before holds good no matter what sort of script you may be writing. The basics of construction, dialogue, characterization, etc. are not arbitrary formulae but, being rooted in human behaviour, are as immutable as the basics of economics or geometry (you can't eat the same cake twice, and things that are equal to the same thing are equal to one another). Certain forms of playwriting, though, have special requirements. The most encountered of these variations is the one-act play.

One mistake – now happily met with less frequently than it used to be – is to look down on the one-act as being merely for amateurs. (Though to consider the amateur market as 'mere' anyway is a big mistake.) The history of the one-act play goes back to the beginnings of English drama. From the earliest plays such as *Abraham and Isaac*, *The Deluge*, *The Shepherds' Play*, or *Everyman* there have been self-contained short pieces. Shakespeare has rustics rehearsing *Pyramus and Thisbe* in *A Midsummer Night's Dream*. Since then Sheridan, Shaw, Barrie, Coward, Priestley, Rattigan, Williams, Wilder, and Pinter have written one-act plays, to name but a miniscule selection from writers who have successfully contributed to this form.

The one-act has appeared in as many guises as there are sorts of play. (With one or two special to itself.) It usually plays for less than an hour, though with some notable exceptions like Schnitzler's *The Green Cockatoo* and O'Neill's *The Emperor Jones*. It can be written in many scenes like Clifford Odets's *Waiting for Lefty* or Coward's *Still Life* or in one scene. It can have several settings as in Galsworthy's *The Little Man* or just one set. The time it covers can be the actual time between curtain rise and fall, or it can cover several generations as in Wilder's *The Long Christmas Dinner*. It can have one character as in Beckett's *Krapp's Last Tape* or fill the stage with characters as in Wilder's *Pullman Car Hiawatha*. The one quality distinguishing it from the rest of drama is the way in which it makes a single gesture. The full-length play will have two or three major crises and climaxes, usually towards the end of each act. The one-acter will build towards just one major climax. It can seldom afford the distraction of a sub-plot.

Having a playing time of less than half that of a full-length play means that the one-act can be much slighter (without being less profound). It can be devoted almost entirely to atmosphere as in many of Maurice Maeterlinck's short pieces: in *The Intruder* (who is Death, intruding into a family circle) a small group sits waiting while a woman in another room is having a baby. Through fitful conversation – 'Are the windows open?'; 'It seems to me the cold is getting into the room'; 'There is a little wind in the garden and the rose petals are falling' – we get the feeling of death coming closer: though in keeping with one of the most basic of rules a big question remains – who will be taken? (In fact it is neither the woman nor the child, but the grandfather.) The one-act play can concentrate on a single character like Krapp or Emperor Jones. It can elaborate on a single joke as in some of Ionesco's absurd pieces (a room filling with furniture until there is only just space for the tenant). It lends itself to experiment: an original idea that may become tedious when stretched to full length can be encapsulated in a short piece – in my *Out of the Flying Pan* two diplomats talk gibberish throughout their negotiations.

Over the last few decades the professional theatre has started to show revived interest in the short play. This is particularly the case with so-called alternative theatre with such fringe activities as lunchtime performances and theatre in education. The main demand though still comes from amateur groups, particularly those entering play festivals.

There have been competitive festivals in the UK since

the British Drama League launched its first in the twenties. Since then they have multiplied, set up by many organizations from Women's Institutes to Young Farmers' Clubs. Rules vary, but the fundamental requirements for festival entries are pretty much alike. Groups are looking for plays which give the best amateur actors and directors the chance to show what they can do – at their best they can be very good – and sometimes those who are not so good can be helped to win by a suitable script.

The first consideration is one of length. Festival rules usually specify a running time of not less than twenty minutes and not more than forty-five minutes. Some may allow entries of up to sixty minutes, but some of the women's organizations insist on no more than forty – and they are a very influential group. A writer is advised to aim at a length of between thirty and forty minutes.

Time also imposes limits on settings. Rules insist that these must be put up in no more than ten minutes and struck in less than five. (Entrants over-running can lose marks.) Box sets (in which the acting area is totally enclosed by scenery) are not usually allowed. This means that the naturalistic domestic interior is the most difficult to cope with.

Allow scope for imagination in setting the play. Not only is a castle or a blasted heath more interesting to look at than an ordinary living-room but it can be suggested more simply on stage. I have seen a Chinese temple created (for *The Golden Fisherman* by F. Sladen Smith – these days a sadly neglected writer) with two vermilion uprights and a large vase of flowers. Moreover when transporting scenery in the back of a car to a festival location a woodland glade is easier to cope with than a sideboard and dining-room suite.

Once that domestic interior has been done away with, ingenuity and inventiveness come into their own, with possible settings from outer space to inside a head. There is nothing more conducive to encouraging dramatic creativity than a bare stage.

Nor is there usually time or opportunity to set up subtle lighting effects, so make sure that your play does not absolutely depend on them.

Costume plays though are very popular, particularly with women's groups, which seem to revel in dressing up. Their popularity may be partly due to the way in which a period dress can disguise a less-than-youthful figure. In addition a costume play can also give the non-performing dressmakers in the group a chance to shine – which may be a deciding factor when choosing a script.

As there are hundreds of Women's Institutes, Townswomen's Guilds, and Ladies Clubs, the all-female market is one to bear particularly in mind. If your play satisfies an all-female cast, its chances of getting a production are likely to be doubled.

When writing for the all-female market special considerations need to be borne in mind. While some groups are able to call upon a large reserve of active members most are not so fortunate. Five or six characters seems to be the most acceptable size of a cast. More may strain resources.

Some festivals have sections for duologues of about ten minutes playing time. These brief pieces seem to be in short supply – perhaps because playwrights are not aware of this potential market. Nor is the demand confined to festivals. Duologues are constantly required for less demanding entertainments such as parties, socials and so on.

When describing characters try not to be too detailed. Descriptions of characters can be taken quite literally by prospective directors. How absurd to have your play rejected because you have given your heroine, say, red hair (which no one in that particular group has) especially if the red hair is quite irrelevant. The same applies to age. As the membership of most all-female groups tends to start in the mid-thirties, describing a character as being in her mid-twenties could cause your play to be turned down. (Even though I have seen a teenaged student admirably played by a WI actress of thirty-five.) Unless a specific age or certain personal peculiarities are absolutely essential, cultivate a diplomatic vagueness in your cast list. Ages can be adjusted to relationships – mother to daughter, twins, etc.

When first considering story-lines about women in

groups, certain stock characters tend to spring to mind. Summed up as 'nuns, nurses and miners' wives waiting at the pit head' they should be approached with caution. Because they are so obvious they will have already been used by generations of writers. Use them yet again and you will be competing against plays which have the advantage of years of festival success behind them.

This caution also applies to certain environments – prison, office, hospital or waiting-room – and to certain situations – the rummage sale, the drama group committee choosing its next play, quarrels at the court of an ageing Elizabeth I. You may have thought of a brilliant twist to one of these, but it should have the something extra that Sue Townsend's *Woomberang* and *Bazaar and Rummage* bring to the hospital waiting-room and the rummage sale.

Many all-female story-lines seem to revolve in some way around the opposite sex. This is not surprising because nature has organized one half of the human race to find the other half of absorbing interest, which can present problems when writing a play with only women in the cast. The more important a male becomes to the plot, the greater will be the demand for him to put in an appearance. Some ingenious devices have been concocted for keeping him in mind while out of sight. He has been confined to the next room – even just behind the door. Sometimes he has just stepped out for a minute, or may even be expected back at any time. He has communicated through letters or by telephone. In my *Funeral Dance* he died just before the play began. In *Smile* a burglar and a photographer are kept just out of view on the other side of the 'fourth wall' where the audience is sitting. Too much ingenuity, though, can draw attention to the fact that the fellow is just not there.

Bear in mind, though, that boy meets girl is not the only story-line. Plots can involve conflict other than friction between the sexes. If gender is not central to the main idea an audience is not so likely to wonder where the men have all got to. Why not write about asserting individuality, defending territory or maintaining status? On occasion I have found it useful to dispense with humans entirely and have written about birds, mice, robots and fairies. As gender (or even age) is irrelevant, this makes for greater flexibility in casting which has been reflected in the number of productions. They have all become some of my most successful plays.

There was a time when all-female groups were considered to be interested only in cup-and-saucer comedies. There may be some still, but overall standards have improved and nowadays many groups are prepared to tackle new forms of staging, complex characters, unusual dialogue and provocative topics. Having said which I must admit that my most popular all-female play of recent years is a costume comedy with lots of tea drinking. The only remaining taboo would seem to be against bad language.

Plays that can be performed with hand-held scripts are also in demand. These can be staged at short notice with little preparation. Moreover as lines do not have to be learned, otherwise active performers who, advancing into the senior citizen class are finding their memories not quite what they were, are able to take part. Bear in mind that, as one hand will be holding a script, action must be carried by the dialogue without too much business or movement.

Young people, in age groups from ten to eighteen years old, also have special requirements. Shakespeare is all very well – with large casts and simple settings he might have been writing for schools and youth groups – but young performers also need plays that are more immediate in their use of language, more contemporary in their awareness of social issues. A gap is waiting to be filled. If it is of any encouragement, my most frequently performed one-act play, Us and Them, was written for the classroom. (A classroom being the space left when desks have been pushed out of the way.) That it did not stay there, but went on to be performed in festivals world-wide, was probably due to the fact that it can be performed by a cast of any number over five, of any age, sex, race or social background.

The festival play and the classroom play have so much in common it is not surprising that from time to time they prove to be identical. To start with there is the limitation of setting. Most major productions are mounted in school halls on stages originally designed for assembly without considering the possibility of being used for putting on plays. With little or no accommodation for naturalism, settings had better be suggested rather than presented in detail. Which means that wider horizons – from jungles to space stations – are actually easier to represent.

A bare stage is always the easiest setting. A bare stage can be anywhere where the words say it is. The action can take place on the roof of Saint Paul's or at the bottom of a treacle well as long as the words conjure up the feeling of the place and the actors sustain the illusion. What is more, the setting can be changed at will, merely by conveying to the audience the information that it has been changed. One of my plays, *The Right Place*, originally written for the classroom, moves from open road to meadow to mountainside to pea-souper fog (in which nobody can see anything) to the bank of a river (across which characters wade) and ends in a fantastic city – all in the course of half an hour.

It is important to provide good parts. And a part means not merely shuffling on as an anonymous part of a crowd, but a character (however simple in outline) that can be acted.

At the younger end of the age range, some performers will be working for the first time with words actually written down. Some may have difficulty even with simple dialogue but will be good at improvisation. Give them a chance to show what they can do. I have found a sort of adaptable chorus to be very useful. This is a group of characters who contribute to the scene using their own words: robots, space travellers, football hooligans, they have been anything that will involve using the imagination.

The best characters and situations are those which the young performers can relate to their own lives, encouraging them to look within themselves for the details of their part.

These details should be brought out rather than imposed. Keep stage directions to a minimum, remembering that everything the writer adds may be blocking something a young actor might have thought of. Try to present the play in broad outline, with no more instructions than are absolutely necessary, so that imaginations can be stimulated. Avoid subtle sub-texts, though. At this stage the actors say what they mean.

Any play should be relevant to the life and times in which it is written, but this applies particularly to those written for young people. If discussion is not sparked or feelings roused, the one question raised by the youngsters is likely to be, 'Why spend all this effort?' Which does not mean that plays should be unremittingly grim investigations into violence, drugs, unemployment and homelessness. Scripts can be as funny as you like, even on such topics as pollution, endangered species, living together and the generation gap. The subject should always be presented in terms of people doing things, not merely talking about them. There is no room for abstract debate. Nothing happening on-stage equals yawns in the audience. Both actors and audience should be encouraged to realize that theatre can be exciting.

Here again there is a demand for duologues. With a duologue two performers can prepare something on their own without supervision. This situation may actually be called for in the syllabus; not to mention entries in music and drama festivals.

After the amateur theatre the single largest market for one-act plays in the United Kingdom is radio.

Every week the BBC puts out plays of thirty, forty-five, and sixty minutes in length, and most of these are original work. Over the years the BBC has made a point of encouraging new writers. Although financial pressures have meant that help and advice are not as readily available as they were once for the promising writer who is still on the brink of a break-though, an unknown with a good play stands as much chance of acceptance as a well-known name.

The only advice is to keep trying. A real writer is one who is never put off by rejection. My first acceptance came only after five years of submitting scripts to radio. Even now I am not sure what made that one more acceptable than the rest, but it was the first of many.

One mistake to avoid, though: a stage script should never be submitted for radio. At least retype it. A radio play should *look* like a radio play. An obvious stage script will be returned unread because the radio drama script unit is looking for *radio* drama. Although this should come as no surprise to anyone, scripts continue to arrive with such instant giveaways as 'When the curtain rises we see ...' or 'He exits down left'. Successful stage plays are frequently adapted for this medium, but such adaptations are always specially commissioned (as are serializations of classic books) and a radio writer has to be really well established before being invited to undertake one.

Try to think in terms of sound. I have read in scripts from beginners such bloomers as, 'Silently the girl faints and without a word a doctor elbows his way through the shouting mob towards her', or 'She enters the empty room through the open door, carefully puts a pile of blankets on the bed and goes out again'. If you can imagine what you have written coming from loudspeaker or headphones, you will avoid mistakes like that.

Laying out the script as radio play from the moment you start to put it on to paper may encourage the right thought processes. A page for radio should look like this:

> (FADE UP BACKGROUND OF SMALL CAFE WITH GENTLE TINKLE OF CUPS AND LOW MURMUR OF VOICES)

EDDIE: This is the place where I first met you, Liz.

LIZ: Don't be gormless. This caff hasn't been built more nor a couple o' years.

EDDIE: There were – a bit of a brook. It ran just about where those tables are now. And there were trees.

LIZ: Shut up, will you? You're worse'n this hangover.

EDDIE: I were just – trying to remind you. Forty years ago. Here. Right here.

LIZ: It don't do no good to remember.
                    (FADE OUT CAFE BACKGROUND)

EDDIE: *(in a whisper)* There was a girl with you. What was her name?

LIZ: Leave me out of it.

VI: *(calling from a distance)* Elizabeth.

EDDIE: Vi. That's it. Vi. Funny kid. She had a pink ribbon in her hair.

LIZ: Blue.

                    (FADE UP COUNTRYSIDE BACK-GROUND. A BIRD SINGS IN A NEARBY TREE AND CHILDREN CAN BE HEARD PLAYING IN THE DISTANCE)

EDDIE: And she were looking for you.

VI: *(approaching)* Liz. Liz. Elizabeth. I'm calling you.

The radio writer uses two elements: sound effects (which can include music) and dialogue. There have been many plays without sound effects but (with the exception of one or two outlandish experiments) none without dialogue. This is the reason why some playwrights consider radio to be the ideal medium. Without their words there can be no radio drama.

Lacking visual aids the words have to create pictures in the listener's mind. If your hero is a one-legged sailor disguised in the costume of a Dagenham Girl Piper, who finds the abducted heroine imprisoned in a Tibetan monastery (radio can conjure up this sort of extravagant setting at no extra expense, even with the required dungeon echo added at the touch of a control) then this must be made clear in words, preferably without the listener being aware that such information is being conveyed. To have the heroine cry, 'Oh, my beloved one-legged sailor, why have you come disguised as a Dagenham Girl Piper to this Tibetan monastery in which I am imprisoned?' is not advised. Incorporate exposition into the action.

Because faces cannot be seen, try to get as much variety as possible into the composition of your cast. Differences in gender, age, social background and even dialect all help to make for easier listening. Female voices in particular tend to present a director with a problem in casting because they can sound so much alike. A gang of schoolgirls or a group of centenarians would equally be a headache.

If strong language should be demanded by character and situation it can be used. But by its very nature a radio play takes place inside the listener's head, playing to an audience of one. The effect of offending words is much greater when addressed to you alone than when shouted across a crowded street. If you feel an expression is absolutely necessary, put it in. But be aware of the effect it is likely to have.

Words are sometimes needed to point up background sounds. Some of these can be perplexingly similar – sea and rain for instance. The BBC's vast library of effects can give you any 'setting' you want with amazing subtlety – I have had a director insert a bee into a summer garden. Ask for a department store and you can choose between Harrods and Woolworths. To point the precise location though – baby wear, books, toys or confectionery – dialogue will be needed. No sounds of bee or spadework could have indicated that my scene was taking place near a shed.

An experienced radio writer should be able to inform the listener unobtrusively. For instance, if one scene ends with, 'All right, then. We'll meet at seven o'clock tonight by the ghost train', and the next scene begins with *Fairground Background* and, 'I'm not late, am I?' we know exactly where we are.

Scenes used to end with 'Fade down': the next scene beginning with 'Fade up', and the slight pause between indicated a change in time and/or place. This is now considered old-fashioned, and the current trend is to cut from one scene to the next, so speeding up the action. Radio can do this with ease, but it can be confusing unless the words make sure that what is happening is crystal clear.

Contrast can emphasize a change of scene; such as following a scene with more or less noisy background with a quieter background – or vice versa. For instance a clock could be ticking in a room after the roar of a traffic-filled street.

Scenes can be very short – as short as one line: radio is the most flexible medium for drama.

Far more flexible than television – writing for which is hardly to be recommended for a beginner: if only because the single play hardly exists in the medium any longer. It has been said that radio producers are looking for plays, while television producers are looking for writers.

One possible way into television for an outsider is via the situation comedy. The idea must extend to a series of at least six episodes (sit. coms. like buses come in groups). Each episode is a twenty-five minute play – in one piece for the BBC, in two parts for commercial television. Original ideas – not reworkings of *Dad's Army, Rising Damp* or *Steptoe and Son* – are welcome. Submit a first episode written in full, with outlines of five others. Keep the number of settings down (four cost twice as much as two) and remember that, the television screen being small, it is not easy to follow more than four characters in a scene. When I was writing for television I was advised that no scene should last longer than a minute and a half, presumably to cater for the attention span of the average viewer. If necessary cut away to another scene. For instance if there are to be separate scenes involving an erring husband and an angry wife show the husband settling for instance in a pub with the girl-friend, cut to wife setting the table for dinner, cut to husband and girl in pub, cut to wife telephoning the office, and so on.

In spite of being a visual medium, television still relies heavily on spoken dialogue to carry information.

Above all else a situation comedy must be funny.

To some extent comedy is like poetry – difficult to define while being instantly recognizable. There seem to be two main elements present in comedy writing. The first and most important is the need to be as truthful as possible. A scene of suspense can become comic if the detail is absolutely truthful. Imagine the opening scenes of *Hamlet* with everyone suffering from streaming colds (those battlements were very chilly); and a successful comedy sketch had Cleopatra dropping the asp down her cleavage, then laughing uncontrollably as the snake wriggled round inside. In Alan Ayckbourn's *Absurd Person Singular* a would-be suicide is constantly being frustrated by the cussedness of domestic appliances, such as a lid that refuses to come off. The situation is potentially tragic, but the true-to-life detail turns it into comedy. An audience will find anything funny it recognizes and can identify with. Which is why references to brand names and well-known people and places tend to raise a laugh.

Poetry has been defined as the right words in the right order (which implies that every word should count) and this certainly applies to playwriting. Mother saying, 'I want this mess cleared up by the time I get back' has a different emphasis from, 'By the time I get back I want this mess cleared up'. Which must be borne in mind when writing comedy. Stress falling on a misplaced word can kill a laugh. Imagine the reply to the old chestnut 'Who was that lady I saw you with last night?' coming as 'That was my wife, not a lady'. Though one of the trials a playwright has to suffer is hearing carefully crafted lines paraphrased by actors. When Noel Coward was rehearsing *Hay Fever* for the National Theatre, Edith Evans insisted on slipping in an extra word that changed the rhythm of a line. Exasperated, Coward protested that he had written, 'On a clear day you can see Marlow' – adding, 'On a *very* clear day you can see Beaumont and Fletcher'.

In his book *The Act of Creation* Arthur Koestler analyses The Joke. Why do we find it funny? The conclusion he reaches is that when two disparate ideas are brought together and the audience makes a connection, the result is laughter. It is rather like the situation when positive and negative electric charges are brought towards each other and a spark flies from one to the other: in terms of comedy that spark is audience reaction. At a low level this accounts for the response to a pun. One word serves two purposes. An example several centuries old – man meeting another carrying a hare asks, 'Is that your own hare or is it a wig?'. The fun – such as it is – comes from the artificial relating of an animal to a hairpiece; but the laugh actually comes when the penny drops, when the listener has also brought something to the joke. This is the reason why, when a joke has to be explained, it ceases to be funny – the work has been done so there is no vital spark. No spark: no laugh. Audiences actually like to work. Many comedians get their effects from what they do *not* say, stopping when they come to crucial words and letting the audience, as it were, run on ahead. When forced to fill in what is missing the audience, leaping the gap, will laugh.

(The principle can work in reverse too. If a line – or situation – is getting a laugh where a laugh is the last thing needed, make sure the audience is not making an unwanted connection.)

There is a demand for very short funny pieces (half a minute to three or four minutes) for both stage and television. Here it is important to know the ending (or punchline) before starting to write, and then work towards it as economically as possible.

With the demise of revue in the West End most of the demand for stage sketches comes from amateur groups (particularly all-female). When writing for television closely observe the programme or personality the material is intended for. In other words study the market.

10   In Business

So you've written a play. Now comes the really difficult part. Arnold Bennett commented that it took less time to write three novels than to get one play on to the stage.

The ambition of most aspiring playwrights is a first night in the West End. Naturally. Aiming for the top is only human nature. The bad news is that, to get up there in lights, an agent is almost indispensable.

This is because a good agent has personal contact with a large number of people influential in the theatre. He knows which managements are in the market for what material and which leading actors are likely to be free in the near future. A play may have to wait a long time before all the right elements come together – the right star, the right director, the right theatre. A mistake in any of these departments can turn even a masterpiece into a flop. Expensively.

The professional theatre is rather like a country town in which everybody knows everybody else. The sort of town where the inhabitants, if not exactly all on friendly terms, at least know what everyone else is doing. Directors and writers working at different ends of the country know each other better than they know their next door neighbours. A good agent will be part of this community.

Some managements even refuse to look at a script that has not been submitted to them through an agent. This is because they know a play must have potential before a reputable agent will agree to handle it. They can rely on that agent's judgement. This does not guarantee that the script will be accepted, but a lot of time is saved by not reading hopeless submissions.

The other bad news for a beginner is that agents are

very reluctant to take on newcomers. Living on a percentage of a client's earnings, an agent will want to be sure that the writer will not only produce a play that will sell, but will go on writing successful scripts. In other words, in order to find someone who will sell your play, you have to prove that it can be sold.

Lists of agents appear in *The Writer's and Artist's Year Book* and *The Writer's Handbook*. These books appear annually, and there should be copies in most reference libraries. When approaching an agency, an initial letter asking if they would be interested in reading your work, might at least avoid unnecessary postage – a heavy script can be expensive.

Don't give up, though. The vicious circle can be broken. An unknown *can* get a play staged; after which agents may be the ones making advances. But first lower your sights. The production will not be on Shaftesbury Avenue.

My first production on the professional stage took place in a small provincial theatre. It was put on in an election week when the Derby was being run, so business was bound to be bad and the manager thought he might just as well lose money on my new script as waste a West End title that might do better. A rail strike and a heat wave helped prove him right. Although nothing else happened to the play, I was thereafter a produced playwright, with some good notices to prove it. What is more I met people who turned up in my professional life afterwards.

Any beginner serious about writing for the theatre should become involved with the theatre. Many of the most successful playwrights from Shakespeare to Orton started as actors. Modern actor/writers include Pinter, Ayckbourn, Coward, Osborne, (not to mention this writer) able to say, person to person, 'I've written this play. Will you read it?'.

However it is not essential to be an actor to get a foot in the door. Cultivate the theatre nearest to you. Some have supporters' societies which may give you an insight into what goes on. See for yourself what goes on there, especially what plays. Experimental work is sometimes given a studio production. (Experimental in this context does not necessarily mean 'weird' – merely that it is an unknown quantity.) If you feel exceptionally sure of yourself, you may be able to snatch a brief word with the director. If you should submit a script after that, at least there will be a face to go with the name on the title page.

Writers' reference books also contain lists of small, fringe companies. Frequently these are touring companies with requirements quite different from those of larger theatres. (I have more than once been commissioned to write a play with no more than three characters.) Working wonders with limited resources and minimal casts (all of which, including the set, have on occasion been packed into the back of a small van) they tend to be more 'committed' than the 'commercial' theatre. What they will not be looking for is another *Mousetrap* or *Run For Your Wife*. Some have a particular point of view to put over – on race or sex or religion or politics. They may commission an idea and then expect the writer to work with the company as the play evolves. To do this, though, you would need some idea of the past work of the company. In other words – back to personal involvement.

There is no way that anyone working with these companies will make a fortune, but those invaluable personal contacts are being established. More than once I have been asked to write a play and the commissioning manager has approached me with such words as, 'You won't remember me, but I was the assistant stage manager when you wrote a play for....' ASMs and small-part players do grow up.

After submitting a play, do not expect a quick decision. The reply you get by return of post will be the play coming back unread. If after six months you haven't heard, a gentle enquiry may be in order. As a theatre director once pointed out to a complaining author, 'This week I am rehearsing the play due to open next week; working on schedules for the one after that; auditioning artistes for the pantomime; working on next year's budget; preparing a submission to the Arts Council for a grant and writing to possible commercial sponsors so that at least there will be sufficient funds to keep the theatre open next year. Which of those activities do you suggest I drop this minute in order to read your play?'

Whatever you do, though, don't spend that waiting time biting your nails. Write another play.

The idea of a production in the West End with the chance of enjoying the tax problems of a Neil Simon or Alan Ayckbourn may be alluring; but are the odds of thousands to one against an acceptance worth so much time and trouble? Especially when, with over a hundred dramatic societies to every professional theatre company, there is no wider outlet for plays than the amateur theatre. Each year thousands of pounds are paid to writers for the plays that are put on by local groups of amateurs. Moreover a really successful piece can go on bringing in a steady income over the years. The W.W. Jacobs classic *The Monkey's Paw* is still being performed over ninety years after its first night.

Plays I have written with specific amateur groups in mind have in fact later been produced professionally on stage, radio and television. Strictly speaking there is no such thing as an amateur play. There are only good plays and not-so-good plays. The fact that a play is put on with unpaid performers by a Women's Institute or youth group rather than staged with stars on Shaftesbury Avenue or Broadway has nothing to do with its quality as drama. The basic principles that make for a good play hold whether for a four-hour epic commissioned by The National Theatre or for a three-minute sketch to be staged at an end-of-term concert.

However it is a good idea to target your play from the very start.

Research for playwriting is very different from that required for articles or short stories, because there are no such clearly defined markets. When writing for magazines one should be able to deduce editorial policy and house style from reading a few issues and targeting contributions accordingly. In the theatre only general trends apply (and even so from time to time a play surfaces that would have seemed dated fifty years ago). However any half-serious playwright will read the *Stage* regularly in order to keep up with what is going on in the professional theatre. In particular this publication keeps playwrights informed on what fringe theatres, provincial repertory, smaller touring companies, theatre in education companies etc. are doing.

It is no bad idea to decide from the outset whether you are writing for the amateur or professional market. To some extent this means asking whether you intend to write a one-act or full-length play. The professional theatre takes very few one-act plays, whereas the amateur theatre is reluctant to stage full-length plays that have not had a professional production. On the other hand the amateur theatre stages so many one-act plays that your chances of getting at least one production are much greater than with a full-length play in the professional theatre. In either case, though, the play should be as good as you can make it. There is no room for shoddy work just because it is aimed at the amateur market: *anything* you write should always be as good as you can make it.

The first contact your play will make with any potential customer – whether theatre-goer or management reader – is the title. It is a selling point. Try to think of one that commands attention, at the same time giving a feeling of the play.

Some titles encapsulate the story-line – *Dead on Nine, The Doctor's Dilemma, I Killed the Count, Ernie's Incredible Illucinations, The Caine Mutiny Court-Martial*; some use the background, especially if it is unusual – *The Shop at Sly Corner, Laburnum Grove, The House of Flowers* (there are a lot of 'house' titles), *The Bird in Hand* (the name of a pub; pub names are almost as popular as houses), *The Dover Road, Our Town*; some pick up a quotation that will strike a chord – *Blithe Spirit, The Owl and the Pussycat, Present Laughter, Journey's End*; some twist a quotation or well-known phrase – *Run For Your Wife, Busman's Honeymoon, Who's Afraid of Virginia Woolf?, How the Other Half Loves*. One of the simplest ways of conveying what the play is about is to name the leading character – *Shirley Valentine, Peter Pan, Julius Caesar, Saint Joan, Sweeney Todd*. The title can also catch the attention by arousing curiosity, as with a sort of puzzle – *Absurd Person Singular, Who Killed Santa Claus?, The Dark at the Top of the Stairs, The Life and Death of Almost Everybody*.

The last of these breaks one general rule of titles: that it should not consist of more than five words. There are sound reasons for this. In the first place the fewer the words the larger the letters can be on promotional material such as posters, newspaper advertisements, handbills – even lights outside the theatre. For another thing, the shorter the title the easier it is to remember. Some eccentric titles have made a point of being extravagantly over-long – *You Know I Can't Hear You When the Water's Running, Oh Dad, Poor Dad, Mama's Hung You in the Closet and I'm Feeling So Sad, The Persecution and Assassination of Marat as Performed by the Inmates of the Asylum of Charenton Under the Direction of the Marquis De Sade*. However as a gimmick this is now rather played out – and anyway those titles were rapidly reduced by the public to *Oh, Dad* and *Marat/Sade*.

Selling a play to the amateur market involves a rather different process from selling to the professional theatre. Amateur groups tend to use acting editions from publishers' lists because those titles are obviously available. In the United Kingdom the dominant company is Samuel French Ltd. Although there are smaller companies who should not be overlooked, French's list, being so much larger than any of the others, is the one most dramatic societies reach for first. (American writers have more choice: in the USA, French have two large and active rivals in The Dramatists' Play Service and The Dramatic Publishing Company.)

It is possible for a full-length play to be published without having had a professional production, but this happens only occasionally.That happened with my *Zodiac* and *The Life and Death of Almost Everybody*, but these started with large, extensively advertised, amateur productions and I already had twenty plays doing well in print. As a general rule a full-length play needs the seal of approval bestowed by a professional showing.

Not so with a one-act play. As relatively few of these are given professional productions and such as are, written mainly for fringe and specialist theatre, not being what the average amateur is looking for, a good unknown play will be carefully considered by a publisher. If it should be placed first in a few drama festivals it does not stay unknown for long. Word gets around. My *After Midnight, Before Dawn* received over fifty productions in its first year of publication, drawing from one adjudicator the complaint, 'I have now seen this play six times in the last fortnight and would be glad not to see it again for another year!'

Personally I like to see a play staged (however indifferently) before submitting it to a publisher. Then I have a chance to correct any obvious mistakes, misunderstandings or staging difficulties. In fact because it will not gloss over any failings, a bad first production may be positively helpful.

Even if a play fails to find a publisher there is still hope for it in the amateur market. As long as scripts are available (and in these days of the ubiquitous photocopier that should present no problem) they can be advertised using small ads in magazines whose readers are likely to be looking for plays. These include *Amateur Stage, Home and Country, The Townswoman* and *Scottish Home and Country*. Each script should state that a licence must be obtained before each performance, and give the address to which applications should be made. A glance at French's current list will give some indication of the going rates for performing fees.

You may be one of the favoured few whose play is accepted by the first person to whom it is submitted. (Blue moons have been observed, pigs have flown and lightning has even been known to strike in the same place twice.) But the history of the theatre is full of instances of successful plays that achieved fame by a stroke of luck, among them *Journey's End, Educating Rita, Loot, The Vortex, Once in a Lifetime*, even *Charley's Aunt*. Can you imagine a management turning down *Charley's Aunt*? Twenty of them did. The first manager to read *Peter Pan* exclaimed, 'Poor Barrie's gone mad!'

Of all the gifts the fairies can bestow on an intending playwright, luck is the most important. There are other important gifts, such as fluency with words, an innate feeling for dramatic structure, the perseverance that can coax a slight spark of talent into something more, and the ability to learn from mistakes. All these dwindle into insignificance compared with luck – the happy chance of being in the right place at the right time. Or at least not being in the wrong place at the time. So much depends on so many people to get one play on to the stage that personally I will only believe a play of mine is going on when I see the final curtain coming down. (The theatre can always catch fire in the interval.)

However there is nothing much anyone can do about luck – except being prepared for it when it happens. Persistence is a great help. As soon as one play is finished, start thinking about the next. James Bridie would be planning his next play while writing the last act of the one before. (Which may be the reason why Bridie wrote so many disappointing last acts.) And remember that, although when competing against several thousand others (BBC radio alone receives about 15,000 scripts each year) your chances of acceptance may not be high, a manuscript in a bottom drawer has no chance at all.

When a script comes back for the umpteenth time, you could read it again in the light of later experience. (Even checking it against some previous chapters.) It is just possible that you may have been doing something wrong. Have you in fact written the play you set out to write, or has Cinderella turned into Ali Baba half-way through without your being aware of it? Is it the right length? Does it fall into that difficult category between sixty and ninety minutes? Or would it take over three hours to stage? Are you making awkward demands such as a cast of twenty and/or a fire engine on stage at the same time? Does your title catch the imagination?

If you are quite sure your play is as good as you can make it, send it out again. And the best of luck to you.

Bibliography

Archer, William *Playmaking* (Chapman Hall 1912)

Ash, William *The Way to Write Radio Drama* (Elm Tree Books 1985)

Baker, George Pierce *Dramatic Technique* (Houghton Mifflin [USA] 1919)

Clark, Barrett H. (Ed.) *European Theories of the Drama* (Crown [USA] 1918)

Cooke, Brian *Writing Comedy for Television* (Methuen 1983)

Egri, Lajos *The Art of Dramatic Writing* (Pitman 1950)

Field, Syd *Screenplay* (Dell [USA] 1979)

Hale, Owen, Marowitz, Charles, Milne, Tom (Eds.) *The Encore Reader* (Methuen 1965)

Hart, Moss *Act One* (Secker & Warburg 1960)

James, Henry *Notebooks* (Oxford University Press 1961)

Johnstone, Keith *Impro* (Methuen 1981)

Joseph, Stephen *Theatre in the Round* (Barrie & Rockcliffe 1967)

Kerr, Walter *How Not to Write a Play* (Max Reinhardt 1956)

Koestler, Arthur *The Act of Creation* (Hutchinson 1964)

Shaw, George Bernard *Our Theatre in the Nineties* (Constable 1932)

Van Druten, John *Playwright at Work* (Hamish Hamilton 1953)

Index